A PENGUIN SPECIAL

S161

THE KINGSHIP OF CHRIST

G. K. A. BELL

The Kingship of Christ

THE STORY OF THE WORLD COUNCIL OF CHURCHES

BY G. K. A. BELL

Bishop of Chichester

PENGUIN BOOKS

Penguin Books Ltd, Harmondsworth, Middlesex

U.S.A.: Penguin Books Inc., 3300 Clipper Mill Road, Baltimore 11, Md
[*Educational Representative:*
D. C. Heath & Co., 285 Columbus Avenue, Boston 16, Mass]

CANADA: Penguin Books (Canada) Ltd, 47 Green Street,
Saint Lambert, Montreal, P.Q.

AUSTRALIA: Penguin Books Pty Ltd, 762 Whitehorse Road,
Mitcham, Victoria

SOUTH AFRICA: Penguin Books (S.A.) Pty Ltd, 218 Grand Parade Centre,
Adderley Street, Cape Town

—

First published 1954

Made and printed in Great Britain
by The Campfield Press
St. Albans

TO

THE MEMBERS OF THE CENTRAL COMMITTEE

OF

THE WORLD COUNCIL OF CHURCHES

TABLE OF CONTENTS

APPENDICES

PREFACE

THE purpose of this book is to give an account of a remarkable movement towards Christian unity which has grown rapidly during the past forty years; and, in particular, to tell the story of how the World Council of Churches (on which all the principal Christian Communions except the Roman Catholic are represented) came into being, and of its far-reaching work today.

A book of this size can only tell a portion of the story, and there is much more that one would like to describe. But I have tried to give a truthful picture of the whole. I have been greatly helped in writing it by many friends. I owe a special debt to Dr W. A. Visser 't Hooft, the General Secretary of the World Council of Churches, who has read each chapter in manuscript, and has both saved me from mistakes and given me the stimulus of his counsel. I have, with his permission, borrowed the title of this book from a work by him published in 1948, before the inauguration of the World Council, and now out of print.

I should also like to express my gratitude to Miss Ruth Rouse for allowing me to see the proofs of her comprehensive and admirable *History of the Ecumenical Movement*. In preparing my book, I have studied the Minutes of Meetings of the Central Committee, and Reports of the Departments and Commissions of the World Council. I have at times embodied some paragraphs from the Reports, without on every occasion specifying the source. I have done this in the interests of both accuracy and of easy reading.

To my Secretary, Miss Mary Balmer, who has typed the manuscript under great pressure, I owe a particular debt. And I am also very grateful to the Publishers and the Printers for their consideration and their speed.

I add four Appendices. There is first a Glossary, indicating some distinctive feature or features in the Member Churches mentioned in the course of this book. This is followed by Diagrams giving certain religious statistics in a broad way. Lastly there is a Bibliography, followed by the Addresses of the Offices of the World Council of Churches.

GEORGE CICESTR:

January 1954

I

THE KINGSHIP AND A
DIVIDED CHURCH

WITHIN the last few years we have had the laws of natural science opened to us with a rapidity which has been blinding by its brightness; and means of transit and communication given to us, which have made but one kingdom of the habitable globe. One kingdom; – but who is to be its king? Is there to be no king in it, think you, and every man to do that which is right in his own eyes? Or only kings of terror, and the obscene empires of Mammon and Belial?

Vexilla regis prodeunt. Yes, but of which king?[1]

Many things have changed since John Ruskin spoke these words at Oxford, in his famous Inaugural Lecture on Art in 1870. Wars between nations have given way to world wars. Discoveries in the field of atomic knowledge have attached a new and grimmer meaning to the blinding rapidity with which the laws of natural science have been opened to us. Distances have been overcome by all manner of new means, both in the form of travel and in the methods of communication. The press, the cinema, the aeroplane, and the radio have each contributed in different ways to the making of the habitable globe much more completely into one kingdom. But the very greatness of these new inventions, and the power which they give for good or for evil, only underline the gravity of the issue. The question 'Who is to be king?' has still to be answered; and on the finding of the true king, and on obedience to him, the destiny of mankind depends.

The answer to which the Christian Church is committed is that the true King is Christ. Indeed it declares that with

1. Ruskin, *Lectures on Art*, Sixth Edition, p. 36.

the birth of Christ in Palestine at the beginning of the Christian era, the reign or kingdom of Christ had already begun. It also declares that although the forces opposing his kingdom are tremendous, his complete victory as King of the whole world will be established beyond all doubt at the end of history. Further, the Christian Church is committed to the service of that kingdom in a unique way. But its effectiveness in that service, and therefore in bringing the message that Christ is the true King home to men everywhere, is most seriously impeded by the divisions within it. The importance of healing those divisions, of bringing the divided parts into the closest possible fellowship or unity, can hardly be overstated. This task, which has always been important, has a greater urgency than ever today. It is the purpose of this book to tell the story of a remarkable movement over a very large part of Christendom in recent years, to come together in a new fellowship in order to proclaim the message of the Kingship of Christ, and the meaning of that Kingship in action.

The Kingdom in the Bible

Before we tell the story of the movement, some brief account of the origin of the Kingdom and its development in the Bible will not be out of place. The doctrine of the Kingdom runs right through the pages of the Bible. It is the doctrine of a King and his people.

God's kingly rule over the entire world that he has made is a present and abiding fact. But this rule is only effectively realized when men in word and deed accept God's sovereignty, and this obligation was assumed by Israel in the covenant at Mount Sinai. Hence, in the Old Testament, the doctrine of the Kingdom is closely linked with the whole ordering of the life of the Israelite nation as an expression of the people's obedience to the divine Law. The association of the Kingdom of God with a concern for moral, political, and social righteousness in the history of a particular community is fundamental to Biblical thought.

But there is something more in the Old Testament picture of the Kingdom. God's rule could only be complete when it was recognized over all the earth and fully accepted by all men. The Israelites did not see this in the world around them and their own history was full of suffering and trouble, disaster after disaster, wandering and exile, apostasy and failure. So the Kingdom came to be associated not only with an existing community but with a hope for the future. Ultimately, God himself would act, and, at the end of history, establish his royal rule over the universe. This hope was held by Israel in many different ways. Often, there was the expectation of a prince visibly ruling the kingdoms of the world, and of a kingdom established in a visible way, with Israel in power and great glory. But, at its highest, the Old Testament pictures Israel as God's servant, chosen for mission as much as for privilege, with the task of proclaiming the coming Kingdom to all nations, and bearing in hope the suffering and evil of the world until the Kingdom should come.

In the New Testament, the hope of the Old is fulfilled. Christ came and announced that the Kingdom in its full sense was at hand. He brings the Kingdom with him. Where he is, it is, and he reigns in God's name. The Kingdom he brought was very different from the earthly power that many of his contemporaries expected, for it was achieved in the very crucifixion of Jesus on the cross. By his death, all the forces hostile to God's rule were deprived of any real power once and for all: his resurrection showed that death itself was no longer the final and negative answer to human existence. The Kingdom and eternal life are one in the New Testament and this is the realm into which men can enter in Christ.

Jesus chose twelve disciples to proclaim that the Kingdom of God was at hand, and this act establishes the foundation and functions of the Christian Church. Significantly, the Church is the New Israel. On the one hand, it is the body of Christ, and therefore the sphere in which men consciously serve the Kingdom and taste the reality of its life. But the Church also has the duty to proclaim the fact of the triumphant Kingdom to all men and to work for its complete realization in all the world. The Church's proclamation of the establishment of a Kingdom of perfect righteousness is based not on an uncertain and imperfect longing, as was that of the Old Israel, but on the sure and certain hope given by the victory of Jesus Christ. Hence the Church is vitally concerned not just with 'religion' or its own existence, but with the whole ordering of human life which it seeks to make an expression of God's will for the world over which he rules.

The Church, then, is not itself the realization of the Kingdom of God on earth. It serves the Kingdom, and is not an end in itself.

In Emil Brunner's words[1] it is 'an essentially imperfect society . . . the Church transcends itself. . . . It can only be understood from the end. To be in the Church is to be oriented toward the final goal. . . . The Church can therefore not be an end in itself; it aims at that which comes afterwards, the Kingdom of God, of which it is only the earthly, historical, hidden aspect in the form of a servant.' And the Church looks forward to the day when the Kingdoms of this world are become the Kingdom of our Lord and of his Christ; and he shall reign for ever and ever. (Revelation 11, 15.)

1. *Das Gebet und die Ordnungen*, pp. 511–2. E.T. *The Divine Imperative*, p. 526.

Divisions in the Church

But the Church charged by its Lord with this mission was one Church. It is now divided. The Church of which S. Paul spoke in his Epistle was one visible Church. There is one body and one spirit ... one Lord, one faith, one baptism. (Ephesians 4, 4–5.) Now there are many bodies of Christians, separated from one another, teaching different doctrines, possessing different ministries, acknowledging different systems of government. There is disunion and division, even conflict and antagonism. Therefore the work of the whole body of Christ suffers. The witness to the Kingship of Christ suffers. Jesus prayed for his apostles and 'for them also which shall believe on me through their word; that they may all be one; as thou, Father, art in me, and I in thee, that they also may be in us; that the world may believe that thou didst send me ... that they may be one, even as we are one; I in them, and thou in me, that they may be made perfect in one; that the world may know that thou didst send me, and lovedst them, even as thou lovedst me'. (John 17, 20–3.) This far-reaching disunion is a terrible obstacle in the way of the world believing 'that thou didst send me'.

Divisions began in the early days of the Christian religion. The distinction between heresy and schism was not altogether simple. But generally speaking heresy means false doctrine, and schism an orthodox sect. Any body which had broken from the Church could be called a schism.[1] Certainly by the end of the fourth century after the birth of Christ a number of bodies were in existence which had broken away from the catholic (or universal) Church. And there is no doubt at all about the grave view taken by the Christian Fathers of the day of the sin of schism. It is an offence against the necessary unity of the body of Christ as laid down

1. S. L. Greenslade, *Schism in the Early Church*, p. 28.

in Scripture. It is also an offence against the paramountcy of Christian love.

I have referred to the early days in the Catholic Church because they are often forgotten or overlooked. But the two principal breaches in the unity of the Church took place later, separated from each other by 500 years. The first breach was between the East and the West, and took place in 1054. It is known as the Great Schism. The grounds for this breach had been prepared long before. There were many reasons brought forward in justification, notably the addition by the Western Church of the words 'and the Son' (viz. the *filioque* clause) to the article in the Nicene Creed which confesses that the Holy Ghost proceeds from the Father. But there were other causes of a non-theological character, national, cultural, political, in which the respective claims of the rival Sees of Rome (for the West) and Constantinople (for the East) became the subject of conflict. The final act which separated the Eastern and Western Churches took place on 16 July 1054, when Michael Cerularius was Patriarch of Constantinople; and the Legates of Rome laid an excommunication in writing on the high altar of the great Church of Sancta Sophia, and departed from it, shaking the dust from their feet and crying 'Let God look and judge'.

The second great breach was the Reformation in the sixteenth century. It was a revolution within Western Christendom against the authority of the See of Rome. It was affected by many circumstances, political, economic, geographical, philosophical. But fundamentally it was concerned with the deepest elements in religion. A reformation of the Church in its head and members was long overdue; and as a result the Western Church was riven in twain, Protestants against Catholics. But the revolution of the Protestants took many forms. In a large part of Germany and in the whole of the Scandinavian countries the Lutheran

Churches emerged, with their doctrine of justification by faith, some with bishops, some without. In France, the Netherlands, Switzerland, and Scotland the Reformed or Presbyterian Churches emerged, under the leadership of Calvin and Zwingli, with Confessions and Synods, but no bishops. In England, where the same abuses and corruptions prevailed as in the rest of Europe, the Church of England underwent a conservative reformation from which it emerged with its Book of Common Prayer, and its combination of Protestant and Catholic factors in a single communion.

These divisions in the Reformation were far-reaching and changed the face of Europe. The Roman Catholic Church outnumbers all other Christian bodies and is strong in all five continents, including both the Americas. In the East, besides the Lesser Eastern Churches which broke away long before the Great Schism, the Orthodox Church, whether Greek (looking to the Ecumenical Patriarch at Istanbul) or Slav (looking to the Patriarch of all the Russias at Moscow) is still the main Christian communion. Since the sixteenth century other Protestant communions have been formed by separation from the parent bodies. In England these are known as the Evangelical Free Churches (i.e. as distinguished from the Church of England by law established) and include the Congregationalists, Baptists, Methodists, together with the Friends and the Salvation Army. And just as the Lutheran, Reformed, and Anglican Churches have spread all over the world, so these post-Reformation Churches, especially the Baptists and Methodists, are found in considerable force in most continents. In the United States they are most numerous of all, and most diverse.

The mere rehearsal of these divisions is enough to show the immensity of the obstacles with which Christian men and women are faced in declaring their witness to the Kingship of Christ in the world today. Although all believe in the divinity of Christ, they are separated from one another by their denominational differences. Although in Christ there is neither Greek nor Jew, barbarian, Scythian, bondman or freeman; and although, the Catholic or Universal Church, so called because it is 'spread throughout the whole world from one end to the other'[1] – is the Church of all nations and classes, Christians are neither united in one Church, nor are they in any sort of position to suppress the evils of nationalism, or to correct injustice in the society around them. No wonder that a movement which seeks to overcome the divisions within the Church, and to draw the various Christian communions together, should be a matter of the highest importance to Christendom as a whole. No wonder that Archbishop William Temple should acclaim this 'world-wide Christian fellowship, this Ecumenical Movement as it has been called, as the great new fact of our era'. Nor should we be surprised that an unusual word should be used to describe it. The word 'Ecumenical', as we shall use it, means both 'world-wide' (literally 'the inhabited earth') and 'that spiritual traffic between the Churches which draws them out of their isolation and into a fellowship of conversation, mutual enrichment, common witness and common action'.[2]

1. J.W.N.Kelly, *Early Christian Creeds*, p. 385.
2. W. A.Visser 't Hooft, *The Meaning of Ecumenical*, p. 28.

LOOKING TOWARDS UNITY

THE scandal of disunity has been felt in all ages by thoughtful Christians of many Churches. There have been a number of efforts of varying significance towards reconciliation or reunion. Some have been by Church authorities, others by individual pioneers. There have been attempts, especially in the centuries immediately after the Great Schism, to reunite East and West; but they have come to nothing. Thought has also been given to the problem of finding a basis on which a Church which had separated from Rome at the time of the Reformation might be restored to communion; but here again with no success. Nor have efforts such as those in the seventeenth century to bring about 'a universal blessed union of all reformed Churches' fared much better. Some Church unions have indeed taken place between Churches of a similar order or doctrine in a particular country. There are also examples of a relationship between different denominations, falling short of union, such as an agreement to allow communicant members of one confession to receive Holy Communion in the church of another confession. But it was not till the twentieth century that a real movement to draw the Churches together on a world scale commenced.

A World Missionary Conference

The first real step forward in this direction arose from the missionary work of the Churches overseas, notably in Africa and Asia. A World Missionary Conference was convened at Edinburgh in 1910. Its purpose was officially defined as 'research and conference regarding missionary work and problems', face to face with all other (non-Christian) religions. But no resolution was allowed to be presented which involved questions of doctrine or Church policy, as to which Churches or societies taking part differed amongst themselves. The Student Christian Movement of Great Britain and Ireland had an important share in the preparations, and some 1,200 delegates, representing the Missionary Societies of the principal Protestant Churches of the world, attended, including delegates from the Missionary Societies of the Anglican Church. A Continuation Committee was appointed, which developed later into the International Missionary Council. And it is remarkable that two of the principal architects of the Edinburgh Conference, John R. Mott (U.S.A.) and J. H. Oldham (Great Britain) and one of the ushers, a young Oxford tutor named William Temple, were destined to play a great part in a later stage of the movement towards reunion, in the formation of the World Council of Churches.

Faith and Order

At this very first stage, the clear connexion between the mission of the Church and the unity of the Church received a powerful testimony. As the Edinburgh Conference closed, Charles Brent, first Anglican missionary Bishop of the Philippine Islands, told the delegates of a new vision which the Conference had given him. It was a vision with a very wide range, for he was clear that the ultimate goal must include the whole of Christendom, with Rome. Three months later, in October 1910, he attended the General Convention of the American Episcopal Church at Cincinnati. He records in his diary that at the early Eucharist on the opening day there came upon him vividly a conviction that a world conference should be convened to consider matters of faith and order. At a great public meeting attended by all the Bishops and Deputies, with delegates from the Women's Auxiliary, he spoke of his vision. Before the Convention closed, on the proposition of the Reverend W. T. Manning, later Bishop of New York, it was unanimously agreed that a Joint Commission be appointed 'to bring about a Conference for the consideration of questions touching Faith and Order, and that all Christian communions throughout the world which confess our Lord Jesus Christ as God and Saviour be asked to unite with us in arranging for and conducting such a conference'. Bishop Anderson of Chicago was elected President, and Robert Gardiner, an influential layman, Secretary. Bishop Brent became a member of the Commission; and thus the project, the most far-reaching of any effort in his crowded life (says his biographer), was launched.[1] It was born in prayer, and every step the Bishop took in promoting it began and ended in prayer. Other Churches in the United States were inspired by the same vision, and appointed co-operating Commissions. Similar Commissions were also set up in Great Britain and Ireland, representing the Anglican, Presbyterian, and Free Churches; and interest spread far and wide, not only in Europe but also in Asia. Deputations to the Vatican and the Orthodox Churches were already planned when the First World War broke out, and all immediate activities in this field had to cease.

The First World War

While the war effectively stopped all immediate plans for an intenser working for a world-wide Christian unity in this field, by its very nature it brought the need for unity home in another way to churchmen with a greater urgency than ever. Already between 1907 and 1913 groups of men in

1. A. C. Zabriskie, *Bishop Brent*, pp. 147–8.

different countries, especially America, Britain, Germany, and Switzerland, had been thinking about the necessity of a new world order founded on a Christian philosophy of life. Churches' Councils for Promoting Friendly Relations between Great Britain and Germany were founded in those countries in 1910. In the United States the Federal Council of the Churches of Christ in America started a similar movement; and the Church Peace Union was formed, Mr Andrew Carnegie handing a very large sum of money to a body of trustees for the general purposes of the peace work of the Churches. A project for a similar Council was set in motion in the Swiss Reformed Churches. Mr J. Allen Baker, M.P., and Mr W. H. Dickinson, M.P., visited France, Belgium, and Germany, and secured the consent of leading members of the Protestant Churches in those countries to take part in an International Conference of Protestants.

Three moments during the next five years stand out as of special importance in linking the movement for Christian unity with the search for international fellowship and peace.

The World Alliance

The first rose directly out of the movement in different European countries and the United States, just described. It was at the very outbreak of the war. One hundred and fifty-three delegates had been appointed by the respective Councils or Committees to attend a conference at Constance. About ninety succeeded in arriving; but they met only to disperse after twenty-four hours. They did however resolve that national committees should be set up, and that an international committee of fifteen members, with power to co-opt, should be established, to maintain co-operation between the national committees. The delegates who returned to London reassembled on 5 August 1914. J. Allen Baker, M.P., was chosen as Chairman, and W. P. Merrill (U.S.A.) Vice-chairman. W. H. Dickinson, M.P., L. Emery (Switzerland), F. Lynch (U.S.A.), F. Siegmund-Schultze (Germany), and J. Dumas (France) were appointed as co-ordinating secretaries. It was decided that the name of the new association should be 'The World Alliance of the Churches for Promoting International Friendship'. It was resolved that the representatives of each nation should form a committee in their own country, and thus gather together a body of earnest Christian men and women who should prepare the way for a world conference of Churches at the end of the war. It was the first meeting of the International Committee, and it was decided that the number of the Committee should be enlarged to sixty. A second meeting was held at Berne in August 1915, with delegates from England, Germany, and Holland, as well as the Scandinavian countries. The name of the organization was changed. It was no longer a 'World Alliance of the Churches' but 'The World Alliance for Promoting International Friendship through the Churches'.

Archbishop Söderblom

Next in time followed an Appeal made in 1917 by the heads of the Scandinavian (Lutheran) Churches, led by Dr Nathan Söderblom, Archbishop of Uppsala, inviting churchmen from both belligerent and neutral countries to meet in conference. None came from the belligerent countries. But a conference of churchmen from neutral countries was held at Uppsala in December 1917. It issued a statement emphasizing the duty of the Church to be the living conscience of nations and of men . . . to employ all its resources in working for the removal of the causes of war . . . to work for international understanding, and to vindicate the sanctity of justice and law in Christ's name, and to demand its further development.

The third moment came with the first meeting of the

International Committee of the World Alliance for Promoting International Friendship through the Churches, in October 1919, at Oud Wassenaar. It was the most significant of all, and must be more fully described.

The Treaty of Peace between the Allied and Associated Powers and Germany had been signed at Versailles on 28 June 1919. Less than three months after this signing, representatives of the principal Protestant Churches in five of the belligerent countries, U.S.A., Britain, Belgium, France, and Germany, and in five neutral countries, Sweden, Denmark, Finland, Holland, and Switzerland, met in the Casteel Oud Wassenaar, near The Hague, to consider how the Churches could best work together for the maintenance of peace. The conference lasted four days (30 September to 4 October). The blockade, Bolshevism, war guilt, the Treaty, missions, were among the themes discussed, in private or public.

A tense situation was caused by a letter written by Wilfrid Monod (France) asking for a declaration by the German delegation that the violation of Belgian neutrality was morally wrong and indefensible, as a condition of the renewal of fellowship within the World Alliance. The German delegates pointed out that no mention of such a condition was contained in the invitation to Oud Wassenaar, and the British delegation supported this plea. One of the Germans, Professor Adolf Deissmann, had already, in November 1918, branded the infringement of Belgian neutrality as an appalling and fateful iniquity; and he and his colleagues, after long consultations with the French and Belgian delegations, decided of their own accord to make a declaration that they personally considered the German violation of Belgian neutrality as an act of moral transgression. The declaration made a profound impression, and led to co-operation in full confidence within the World Alliance between the Germans and the rest.

But the subject which proved by far the most absorbing was a proposal for a World Conference of Churches on moral and social questions. Dekan O. Herold, President of the Swiss Church Federation, introduced the matter to the conference, and the General Secretary of the Federal Council of American Churches, Dr C. S. Macfarland, and Archbishop Söderblom, on his proposal, were invited to present a memorandum for discussion. It was Archbishop Söderblom who was its most conspicuous champion. Elected Archbishop at the outbreak of war, at the age of 48, Nathan Söderblom was a brilliant scholar, a remarkable linguist, and an eloquent speaker. Alert, vivacious, he was a man of unquenchable spirit, going here, there and everywhere among the delegates, a figure of medium height, with a fine head and a mass of brown hair, wearing a black frock-coat and trousers, a gold cross on his breast, a white tie, and a big black felt hat. He was the most vivid personality in the company. But as he was an unusual kind of Archbishop, so the proposal was a very novel one, and met many objections. Who should be invited? Should it be confined, as some desired, to Protestant Churches? Should it, as Anglicans asked, include representatives of the Orthodox Churches? Or – more daringly – Rome? Where should it be held? Who should issue the invitations? Should it be sponsored by the Churches as such? or by the Swiss, or American, Federal Councils? or by the World Alliance? The discussion was prolonged. In the end the International Committee passed a resolution expressing its deep sympathy with the general proposal. It considered however that the organizing of such an official Church conference lay beyond the competence of the World Alliance, and referred the resolution to the national committees of the World Alliance, requesting them to communicate it to the ecclesiastical authorities in their respective countries.

It was a cautious, but a genuine, beginning. It led to a

preparatory meeting at Geneva in 1920, attended by ninety members from different countries, and visited by a commission from the Orthodox Church. The visit of the Orthodox commission was significant. The Ecumenical patriarchate at Constantinople had for some time been giving its attention to the possibility of a closer intercourse and a mutual understanding between the several Christian Churches, in spite of the doctrinal differences existing between them; and issued an Encyclical Letter 'To all the Churches of Christendom' on the subject of fellowship and co-operation, in January 1920, considering the matter both feasible and timely 'on the establishment of the League of Nations which has now been effected with good omen'.

I have given this fuller description of the Oud Wassenaar meeting because it was the decisive event in those early days; for it was there that the project of a World Conference of Churches on moral and social questions, under the title 'Life and Work' (as distinguished from 'Faith and Order'), began to take effective shape.

The Stockholm Conference

It is not necessary here to recount the stages which, after many meetings and consultations, and much prayer, led to the World Conference of the Churches held at Stockholm in August 1925. Beyond doubt this Conference was a landmark in the history of the Christian Churches since the Reformation. Rome was not represented. Alike in the preparation and the conduct of the Conference, Archbishop Söderblom was the moving spirit. Without him it could never have happened. It was not only his vision, but his abounding vitality, his powers of persuasion, his leadership and inspiration, that made Stockholm possible. No one who was not in touch with authoritative Church opinion at that time can at this distance easily understand how difficult it was to convince the leaders of the Churches of the need of coming together, for a purpose difficult to translate into very concrete terms, in this necessarily dramatic way. At the same time the achievement would not have been possible at all at that date without the strong support given in various ways by the World Alliance for Promoting International Friendship through the Churches.

On the administrative side Dr Henry Atkinson (U.S.A.) as General Executive Secretary, and Dr Adolf Keller (Switzerland) as Associate Secretary, gave untold help. The Church and people of Sweden were most generous in their hospitality. The Church Peace Union (U.S.A.), owing much to Dr. Atkinson's guidance, made immense contributions to the expenses of the conference, the preliminary regional meetings, and the travelling expenses of many delegations.[1]

The Conference, known as the Universal Christian Conference on Life and Work, dealt with a large number of contemporary questions, international, racial, social, educational. Worship played a prominent part in the proceedings; and the Church of Sweden held a Communion Service in Engelbrekt church on Sunday, 23 August, at which churchmen of many communions received the Sacrament.

There were over 600 delegates, from thirty-seven countries. A strong Orthodox delegation included the Patriarch Photios of Alexandria, and Archbishop Germanos of Thyateira (who was to be a leading figure for many years to come). The Germans sat in a solid block by themselves, still feeling their isolation. There were hardly any delegates from the younger Churches in Asia and Africa; but the Churches of the older countries were well represented. Among the delegates who provided a link with the World Alliance was Bishop Ammundsen of Denmark. He had special experience

1. The Church Peace Union contributed 176,005.73 dollars to the Universal Christian Council from 1921 to 1933. (From statement by the auditors of the C.P.U. in 1943, supplied by Dr Atkinson.)

in the work of conciliation, as his diocese included both Germans (as a result of the war) and Danes. Humorous, devout, an excellent linguist, he never failed in his words of wisdom and his attitude of friendship. William Adams Brown (U.S.A.) was another of those who took a leading part both at Stockholm and after. He was one of the best-known theologians in the United States, with a zeal for unity, a courteous manner, and a great desire to find a way of bringing opposed points of view to concord. These two, with Dr A. E. Garvie (Britain), W. Monod (France), Archbishop Germanos (Greece), Dr Siegmund-Schultze (Germany) and myself, were formed into a group to draft a Message. This was the only act of the Conference, and it cost many heart-searchings before it was completed. In the end, Siegmund-Schultze had to give way to Deissmann, as representing the Germans; and Monod, Deissmann, and I were left together to produce a final shape. Various suggestions were made. There was some fear lest the Message should be too liberal in its general attitude. In my diary I noted that 'Ihmels was constantly darting in with very conservative and timid suggestions – very much afraid of a "United Church" – of appeals to youth, workers, and teachers, unless you limit the appeal to Christians in each category!' There was great discussion as to what might be said on the social question. 'Could it be strengthened?' said the friends of labour. 'Could it be weakened?' said the employers – holding two special meetings to discuss it. In the end, after visits to the printer at two o'clock in the morning, the Message was ready for noon on 29 August, and on the whole very well received. It was carried, with four dissentients, all dissenting on the ground that it did not go far enough on the peace question.

At the conclusion of the Conference a Continuation Committee was appointed to carry on the work.

The Lausanne Conference on Faith and Order

While the Life and Work movement was gaining in strength, the earlier parallel movement known as Faith and Order was also active, and many churchmen of different nations took part in both. It too marked a step forward in mutual understanding. One particularly encouraging action was the unanimous adoption by delegates of the 'Call to Unity', followed by the receiving *nem. con.* of 'The Churches' Message to the World'. Further discussion of its place in the three World Conferences on Faith and Order is reserved for the chapter dealing with that subject. As with Life and Work, so with Faith and Order, a Continuation Committee was set up.

Each World Conference as it met registered an advance in the ecumenical movement. It is well to note that the chief value of these conferences lies in the personal contacts which they enable delegates to make on a world-wide scale, and in the inspiration which they give not only to those attending, but to the many in the Churches at home when they hear reports from the delegates after their return. Public meetings at the time, resolutions or messages adopted by a world conference, have their uses. But it is the encounter of delegate with delegate, or of individual churchman with individual churchman, that matters most; together with the general kindling of the spirit which is so clearly perceptible at a conference that has been wisely planned. Conferences, therefore, are a means to an end, not an end in themselves. They are places where a spiritual exchange can begin, where there may be communion and prayer and devotion, and knowledge can be gained of other ways and confessions, and other kinds of approach to God and the world. They also bring home in an altogether unforgettable way to those attending for the first time the universal character of the Church. Similarly the great contribution made by the Con-

tinuation Committees in the total development comes from
the means which their regular meetings provide for mutual
understanding amongst leaders and theologians in the different Churches. Trust grows up through the succeeding
years, and a deep spiritual fellowship is created.

National Socialism and the Church

A new impetus, however, was given to the ecumenical
movement by the rise of the National Socialist State in
Germany in 1933. It was the Life and Work side which was
most strongly affected. Meeting at Novi Sad, Yugoslavia, in
September 1933, as the guests of Bishop Iriney, a saintly and
devoted Orthodox advocate of Christian Unity, the Executive Committee of what had now become the Universal
Christian Council for Life and Work felt obliged to record
grave anxieties 'in particular with regard to the severe
action taken against persons of Jewish origin, and the serious
restrictions placed upon freedom of thought and expression
in Germany'. It authorized me as its chairman to make
direct representations to the new head of the German
Evangelical Church, Reichbischof Müller.

When the Universal Christian Council itself met at Fäno
in Denmark in August 1934 the situation had become
worse. There was an extraordinary scene when a Nazi
courier came by air from quarters attached to the new
government in Germany, with instructions to the German
Church delegates. The whole atmosphere of this meeting
was tense, as there were anti-Nazi Germans secretly present
as well as official delegates of the Evangelical Church. Discussion in closed sessions was exceedingly animated, reports
somehow reaching the outside world through American
press agencies, and causing a great stir.

The Council expressed its criticism of the Nazi regime in
clear terms. Strong support was given to the resistance move-

ment in the Confessional Church; and while the Council also expressed its desire to remain in friendly contact with all groups in the German Evangelical Church, it added Praeses Wurm and Pastor Dietrich Bonhoeffer to its membership as a special sign of its resolve to maintain close fellowship with the Confessional Church. More important than this, the Council decided, on the initiative of Dr J.H. Oldham, that in the light of the great extension of the functions of the State everywhere, and the emergence in some countries of the authoritarian or totalitarian State, the attention of the Churches must be directed to the problem of Church, Community, and State, and the conflict between Christianity and secularism. It is no exaggeration to say that it was the acute conflict between the Church and the State, now so clearly perceived, that gave the main direction to the future character of the ecumenical movement on its Life and Work side.

The Oxford Conference

Oxford was the scene of the second World Conference on Life and Work in 1937. It took 'Church, Community, and State' as its theme. It was exceedingly well prepared in advance; and it was greatly strengthened on the Church and State side by the presence of leaders in the public life of various countries, such as Lord Robert Cecil, Max Huber, and John Foster Dulles. The problems were graver than those which Stockholm had faced, and the whole international situation was far more serious. There were fewer Orthodox delegates, but there was a considerable increase in the representation of the younger Churches, especially from China and Japan. Christian unity above national frontiers was vividly expressed when we saw Chinese and Japanese delegates were seen sitting side by side in the conference hall, in Christian fellowship, while the evening papers outside displayed the headline, 'Japanese planes bomb Chinese villages'.

The delegation from the German Evangelical Church had been forbidden to come; but the Conference sent it a special message of fellowship. It was, it said, 'greatly moved by the afflictions of many pastors and laymen who have stood firm from the first in the Confessional Church for the sovereignty of Christ, and for the freedom of the Church of Christ to preach His Gospel'.

Dr John R. Mott, chairman of the Business Committee, presided over many sessions. Dr J. H. Oldham was chairman of the Research Commission charged with the preparatory work for the Conference. Archbishop William Temple drafted the Message which was ultimately adopted. The Presidents were the Archbishop of Canterbury, Archbishop Eidem (Sweden), Archbishop Germanos (Greece), Professor Adams Brown (U.S.A.), Pastor Boegner (France), and (the first occasion on which a representative of the younger Churches took such a leading position) Bishop Azariah (India). There was a strong Youth delegation. Services of Holy Communion were held at St Mary's and St Aldate's at which the Archbishop of Canterbury and I were the celebrants, and all the delegates were invited to receive Communion.

The World Council in Process of Formation

A few weeks later another World Conference on Faith and Order met at Edinburgh, as will be described in Chapter 10. But a significant decision was reached at both World Conferences, the result of the findings of a Joint Commission which had been set up by agreement to review the work of ecumenical co-operation, and to make recommendations regarding future policy.

It had been evident for some time that if the Churches

were to give adequate support to the ecumenical cause, both Faith and Order and Life and Work ought to join together in a single movement, working through distinct and safeguarded departments. Amongst the considerations which supported the plan of a World Council of Churches were the following: (1) the difficulty of obtaining support for two separate movements; (2) the belief that no division of territory between faith and practice could be maintained; (3) the need of associating the Churches themselves more closely together, and drawing them into unity, always against a background of world evangelization; (4) the need of winning the interest of youth. Both Conferences voted in favour, though opposition was expressed by Bishop Headlam at Edinburgh, for fear that 'the new Council would pass resolutions on public affairs, and so do great harm'.

A Constitution for the World Council was agreed in 1938 by a Joint Committee of fourteen, with the assistance of an Advisory Conference which met at Utrecht. A Provisional Committee was set up, to be responsible for all work preliminary to the meeting of the First Assembly. Archbishop William Temple was elected as its Chairman; and Dr W.A. Visser 't Hooft was appointed General Secretary. Invitations were sent to the Churches in the autumn of 1938. Links were established at the Tambaram Conference in India between the International Missionary Council and the World Council. The Provisional Committee, at a meeting at Saint-Germain in January 1929, provisionally fixed August 1941 as the date for the First Assembly. But once again preparations for this new and great advance in Christian unity were interrupted by war.

3

THE TEST OF THE SECOND
WORLD WAR

THE attitude of the Churches in the belligerent countries towards one another when the Second World War broke out was very different from the attitude of the same Churches when the First World War began. The fact that the tyranny of Hitler's regime found its victims in the Evangelical and Catholic Churches in Germany, as well as in the Jewish race; and that from 1933 onwards the Confessional Synod of the Evangelical Church, and the Roman Catholic Church, had resisted the regime, no doubt made a big difference to Christian opinion in U.S.A., in Britain, and in other countries of Europe. There was not the same temptation to identify the Church with the Nation as there had been in 1914. But there is also no doubt that the new sense of the spiritual bonds between Christians of different countries to which the ecumenical movement had given birth had a profound influence on Church leaders of both sides. In Visser 't Hooft's words, 'It must and can be said that when total war came the great majority of the Church leaders did not forget their obligation to the Lord of the Church, and their obligations to their fellow-Christians'.

The Message of the Oxford Conference of 1937 had included the words, 'If war breaks out, then pre-eminently the Church must manifestly be the Church, still united as the one Body of Christ, though the nations wherein it is planted fight each other, consciously offering the same prayers that God's Name may be hallowed, His Kingdom come, and His will be done in both, or all, the warring nations. This fellowship of prayer must at all costs remain unbroken'. What was the duty of the World Council of the Churches (in process of formation) in time of war?

Deepening of Ecumenical Fellowship

A meeting of the Administrative Committee (an organ of the Provisional Committee) was held at Apeldoorn in Holland in January 1940, to consider what the Provisional Committee could profitably do. Pastor Boegner and M. Guillon (France), R. S. Barnes (U.S.A.), Archbishop Temple, W. Paton, H. Carter and the Bishop of Chichester (England), Professor Gulin (Finland), Dr Koechlin (Switzerland), together with Archbishop Eidem (Sweden), Bishop Noack (Denmark), and W. A. Visser 't Hooft, arrived to confer. Bishop Berggrav had also come from Oslo, to see what encouragement he and his Scandinavian colleagues could get from churchmen of different countries in favour of mediation between the warring Powers. There was much grave discussion on this point outside the meeting of the Administrative Committee itself; and a statement was drawn up by Archbishop Temple to which the four British participants gave their signatures, setting out the conditions under which in their opinion negotiations could be opened. These included an undertaking to recognize the Czechoslovak and the Polish peoples as independent and sovereign; and a requirement that as part of the new order 'a prominent place must be given to economic justice and to the enterprise of making available for the well-being of all peoples the wealth which science now enables mankind to produce in so great abundance'. It should be added that Bishop Berggrav, who had been courteously received at the Foreign Office in London before going to Apeldoorn, got no hearing at all when, after Apeldoorn, he went to Berlin.

The Administrative Committee itself, however, was concerned with the task of the World Council. There were wide differences of opinion. Some members hoped that the Churches would make a declaration on basic issues at stake concerning aggression and freedom. Others pressed that the Churches should do all in their power to keep the door open for mediation. No agreement could be reached on a common statement: but the meeting of the delegates, and the exchange of ideas had very great value. It was arranged to continue the discussion by correspondence. In May 1940 total war began, and further communications were impossible.

The World Council of Churches, however, was very much alive. And although the Geneva staff was reduced, and responsible committees were unable to meet, there was an actual deepening of ecumenical fellowship. It took various forms. For example, links were maintained between Geneva and the Confessional Church in Germany. Dr Hans Schönfeld, a German subject resident in Geneva and in charge of the Study Department, risked his life many times by repeated journeys to Germany, the occupied countries, and to Sweden, in order to keep in touch with the various Churches. There was one famous occasion in May 1942 on which Hans Schönfeld from Switzerland and Pastor Dietrich Bonhoeffer from Berlin came separately to meet me in Stockholm whither I had gone to renew old contacts with Church leaders in Sweden. Their arrival was a great surprise. Nor did either know that the other was coming. I had long, intimate talks with each as well as with both together. They told me in great detail about the character and purposes of the German Resistance. Pastor Bonhoeffer also secretly gave me the names of the leading personalities – the same who ultimately were involved in the Hitler plot of 20 July 1944. They wanted me, if I could, to find out from the British Government whether, if the whole Hitler regime were overthrown, the Allied Governments would be willing to treat with a new *bona fide* German Government for a peace settlement. Various suggestions were made as to how the Allies, if they were willing, might make their attitude known whether by public announcement or otherwise. I emphasized the need of declaring German repentance and this was accepted. I also spoke of the importance of the Allied Armies occupying Berlin. Schönfeld agreed that such occupation would be a great help for the purpose of exercising control. I was with them for many hours and Bonhoeffer felt in particular 'there must be punishment by God – our action must be understood as an act of repentance'. I reported the conversations fully to Mr Eden when I got home but the Government decided that no action could be taken. It was a sensational experience for a Churchman in wartime, but it was an act of very great bravery on the part of the two Germans. It was a very definite attempt to secure an earlier peace. It would never have been made had there been no ecumenical movement. To the great loss of Germany as well as the ecumenical movement, Dietrich Bonhoeffer was murdered by the S.S. in April 1944, after two years in prison. Hans Schönfeld has for many years now been isolated from his friends by a grave psychological illness.

There was a continual stream of information of many kinds through the World Council Offices. This was passed on to the Churches through the Ecumenical Press Service, or in less official ways. The wireless proved a very great help by way of giving news to churchmen in different countries. The sense that the World Council of Churches and the individual members of the Provisional Committee remembered and prayed for them gave great courage to the heroic martyrs in the concentration camps of the Third Reich, and in Nazi-occupied countries. Every Christmas, I was asked to make a special broadcast to churchmen in Germany.

'In these last years,' said Bishop Berggrav, preaching in the Protestant Cathedral at Geneva on the occasion of the first meeting of the Provisional Committee after the War

(February 1946), 'we have lived more intimately with each other than in times when we could communicate with each other. We prayed together more, we listened together more to the Word of God, our hearts were together more.' And since one example is worth a thousand general statements, I reproduce, with his leave and in his own words, Bishop Berggrav's own experience of a remembrance by Archbishop Temple in the middle of the war:

I was confined in my cottage in the woods in Asker. I had 17 policemen on guard of which 3 were on duty at a time. A peasant's wife had the idea to bring me every day a bottle of milk. The guards were accustomed to her coming, but she was of course only allowed to go as far as to the fence, where the guard then took over the bottle. This day she didn't walk the path, but came through the forest, jumped the fence and was before my kitchen window before the guards observed it. She whispered to me in a hurry: 'My husband listened to London yesterday evening, and he heard the Archbishop of Canterbury pray for you, bishop!' Then the guards arrived and took her away, but what a difference with me! No longer left alone, but taken into the fellowship of Christian brethren, even in Great Britain. This moment is my deepest experience of 'Ecumenism' as a reality.

Two other forms of ecumenical fellowship which continued right through the war had a very special value. They concerned refugees from Nazi tyranny, and prisoners of war.

Service to Refugees

In January 1939 the Provisional Committee, at its first full meeting at Saint-Germain in France, had to face the challenge of the increasingly tragic situation of the refugees. It appointed Dr Adolf Freudenberg to take charge. He was a German diplomat by training. He was then ordained as a pastor. But he was himself a victim of the Nazi discrimination against non-Aryans. He and his family formed a part of a considerable body of German pastors and their families who had found refuge in Britain on my invitation backed by the Church of England Committee for non-Aryan Christians at Christmas 1939. His first duty was to co-ordinate the work of the various national Christian Committees for Refugees. When war broke out he was in Switzerland, and was therefore able to keep in touch with the various countries in which the refugee situation became increasingly acute, and to organize the administration of spiritual and material aid. At first his chief task was to help as many non-Aryan Christians as possible to emigrate from Germany. With the fall of France came a new and more difficult call. Thousands of non-Aryans were deported from Germany to southern France. French Protestantism rose to the challenge. Young Christians, under the direction of Mlle Madeleine Barot, and the Chaplaincy Service to Refugees, with strong backing from ecumenical resources, did everything in their power to lighten the misery of the refugees in the camps. Later on, when the refugees were being sent back to the death camps in the East, French pastors, priests, and youth leaders risked everything to get German non-Aryans across the mountains and barbed wire into Switzerland, where they were helped from funds supplied by the Churches of Switzerland, U.S.A., and Sweden. Other refugees in Italy, Hungary, and Shanghai were also supported from ecumenical funds.

Service to Prisoners of War

Soon after the outbreak of war, plans were set on foot to help those taken prisoner. This work has been described as the most visible expression during the war of the World Council of Churches' life. The Ecumenical Commission for the Chaplaincy Service to Prisoners of War was organized in 1939. In order to have the maximum freedom in its negotiations with the belligerent Governments, it was constituted as an independent body. But it was in fact an organ of the Council. Dr Koechlin of Switzerland became its first President. The main activities began in the summer of 1940, when the great stream of prisoners of war flowed to the camps in Germany. Contacts were made with the 'Hilfswerk für Deutsche Kriegsgefangene und Internierte' which was mainly organized to serve German P.O.W.s, but was able and ready to render assistance to the work for prisoners of war in the camps in Germany. The Vice-chairman of the Commission, Professor Jacques Courvoisier of Geneva, made four visits to the camps in Germany from 1940 onwards. These visits helped the Commission to define its policy. One of the main tasks was to negotiate with the authorities concerning the most effective distribution of the available chaplains so that at least all larger camps should have pastoral service. In very many cases, however, no chaplain could be provided and laymen had to take charge of the congregation.

In addition to this the Ecumenical Commission organized a regular supply of books, brochures, vessels for the Holy Communion, and the like. With the help of the American Bible Society a constant stream of Scriptures was received. From 23,000 in 1940 the number of Scriptures sent annually rose steadily to 126,000 in 1945. Christian literature had also to be specially written: and a number of well-printed brochures, with fine illustrations, were sent out at the time of the main Christian Festivals. From 1945 onwards the Commission also issued a paper, 'Die Lager-Gemeinde'. Much help was also given to prisoners through personal correspondence.

Similar action was taken in P.O.W. camps in North America, and in Britain. There was a close association with the Y.M.C.A. in the North American camps. The Swedish Churches were also well to the fore in supplying chaplains. It is no exaggeration to say that the prisoners of war were constantly surprised to find that the Church followed them with its ministry to a foreign country and behind barbed wire. It is not claimed that the whole ground was covered; but a great effort was made, and the Governments concerned were usually ready with full facilities. In the whole work of this ecumenical ministry the Churches of different countries, particularly the American, Swedish, and Swiss Churches, with the help of the American Bible Society, the International Red Cross, and the World Committee of Y.M.C.A.s, gave ungrudging service to prisoners through and with the World Council of Churches.

Christian Reconstruction in Europe

Side by side with the ministry to the refugees, and the visiting of the prisoners, plans were also being made to provide help in the task of reconstruction for Churches which would need it most. The Central Bureau of Inter-Church Aid, founded by that great ecumenical churchman Dr Adolf Keller at the time of the First World War, had already done pioneering work of a notable kind on an increasing scale. It was recognized right in the middle of the Second World War that if the World Council of Churches was to be true to its ideal as a fellowship of the Churches, an organization would be necessary to give effect to that fellowship among the Churches which had suffered through occupation, or because of foreign oppression. Dr S. McCrea Cavert, General Secretary of the Federal Council of the Churches of Christ in America, had paid a visit to Geneva in September 1942, just a few weeks before the total occupation of France made further journeys of this kind impossible, to discuss the question of post-war reconstruction on behalf of the American Churches. Projects were prepared, and there was consultation as far as possible with Churches in the receiving countries, as well as in U.S.A. and Britain.

The *raison d'être* of the Reconstruction Department was

defined by the General Secretary of the Provisional Committee in July 1943 in the following memorandum:

The paramount principle is that which is implied in the very existence of the World Council, namely that the task of reconstruction is to be conceived as an ecumenical task in which all the Churches participate to the limit of their ability, and that the common objective is to rebuild the life of the whole fellowship of Churches which finds expression in the World Council. If this ecumenical principle is taken seriously, this will mean that the Churches will agree to co-ordinate their policies and activities in order to make certain that all needy Churches receive adequate help, that the Churches will not confine their help exclusively to the Churches belonging to the same denomination or confession, and that the autonomy and desires of the receiving Churches are taken in full consideration.

A preparatory committee, under the chairmanship of Dr A. Koechlin, was set up in Geneva on 25 May 1944. The new World Council Department, and the Central Bureau of Inter-Church Aid, with full help from Dr Keller, worked together on lines which led to their ultimate fusion. Inquiries were made into the needs of the Churches, preliminary reports having been received from France, Germany, the Balkans, and Holland. Reports also came from Britain, U.S.A., Sweden, and Switzerland as to the beginning of national Inter-Church Reconstruction committees; and possible relations with UNRRA were discussed. By December 1944 Dr J. Hutchison Cockburn of Scotland had accepted the post of Senior Secretary of the new Department. The first meeting of the Department properly so called was held on 15 May 1945 – a meeting made notable by the intimation of a gift of 100,000 dollars from the New York office of the Central Inter-Church Aid. But of the gifts, plans, and projects more will be told as our story proceeds.

4

THE EARLY POST-WAR YEARS:
1945–1948

THE war in Europe ended in May, and the war with Japan in August 1945. Immense problems immediately confronted Churches as well as Governments in all parts of the world. But the leaders of the Churches had an advantage denied to Church leaders after the First World War. There was a World Council of Churches in process of formation, with a staff, an office in Geneva, and some limited funds.

The General Secretary and other members of the staff found it possible to travel. As countries were liberated, Inter-Church Aid Committees were formed, and took joint counsel. Visits were paid by one or other of the Secretaries of the Department of Reconstruction and Inter-Church Aid to France, Belgium, Holland, Norway, Finland, Germany, Austria, Czechoslovakia, Poland, and Hungary, as well as to all the giving countries – which included Denmark. In October 1945 Dr Michelfelder, a Lutheran from the U.S.A., agreed to act as the temporary Director of a new Division of material aid. 600,000 dollars were made available by the American Churches for the buying of supplies, and considerable quantities of goods were offered by the Churches of U.S.A., Sweden, and Switzerland. In October 1945 the European Central Office was finally fused with the new Department, which added 'Inter-Church Aid' to its original title in order to make it clear that it was the inheritor of a great labour and a high tradition, formed under the inspiring leadership of Dr Adolf Keller.

By February 1946 the Provisional Committee was informed that the World Council Services Committee in the U.S.A. had set up a provisional four-year budget of 9,000,000 dollars, and that a large part of this had already been received from the co-operating Churches, and passed on to the Department, or directly to the needy Churches. The Swiss Reconstruction Committee had raised and spent its first million francs, and was appealing for its second million. The British Committee for Reconstruction in Europe had received considerable funds from the VE-Day collections, of which it had spent as much as the transfer situation allowed. The Swedish Committee had raised substantial sums for the sister-Churches in Norway and Finland, but had also given relief to Holland and Germany. A specially encouraging individual gift had been that of Mr John D. Rockefeller, who had put 500,000 dollars at the disposal of the World Council Services Committee for reconstruction work in Europe.

A Delegation to the German Church

There was another action of great importance taken by the World Council of Churches (in process of formation) in the early months after the war. At meetings in New York and London in the spring of 1945 it was decided to hold a full meeting of the Provisional Committee in Geneva the following February. It was clearly most desirable that the meeting should be truly representative. One of the first steps, therefore, which the officers of the Provisional Committee were bound to take was to get into touch with the new leadership of the German Evangelical Church. The position of that Church was greatly clarified when a new Council of twelve was appointed in the summer, composed of men who had led the Church in its struggle against National Socialism. In October a strong delegation from the Provisional Committee, including Pastor Boegner and

Pierre Maury (France), Dr Kraemer (Holland), Dr Cavert and Dr Michelfelder (U.S.A.), Dr Koechlin (Switzerland), Dr Visser 't Hooft, myself and the Reverend E. Gordon Rupp (Britain) went to Stuttgart to meet the new Council. When it arrived its members did not know whether it would be possible to find common ground. It was true that relationships had been maintained between the World Council of Churches and a number of leaders of the Confessional Church. But would it be possible to arrive at such a deep and wide reconciliation that the Churches of Germany and those from the Allied Nations could again co-operate with mutual confidence? Had not the question of war guilt hung like a heavy shadow over the ecumenical movement in the decade after the First World War?

The meetings were opened on 18 October by a public service of worship in the Markuskirche. Dr Martin Niemöller preached. When the delegation heard his sermon they felt a great sense of relief. For its whole burden was that the German nation, and the Church as part of the nation, could only cry to God for forgiveness that it had been implicated in so much wrong-doing. Then when the actual discussion started Dr Asmussen made a short but very substantial speech. He said that we ought to talk with each other as standing before God, that is 'as if God only existed'. It might be dangerous to say this, for it might be used for propaganda purposes, but it *had* to be said: 'forgive us'.

When that word had been spoken and confirmed by others all obstacles to renewed and stronger fellowship were removed. Dr Kraemer who had been a leader of the spiritual resistance in Holland, and had been in a concentration camp, could say that precisely those who had suffered much did not feel inclined to harsh judgement. 'We are not to measure the guilt of every Church or nation. We stand together as Christians and to reconstruct Europe together.'

The next morning (19 October) Bishop Wurm, Bishop

Dibelius, Bishop Meiser, and the rest of the Council brought the following Declaration which had been prepared overnight:

The Council of the Evangelical Church in Germany, in its meeting of October 18–19 in Stuttgart, greets the representatives of the World Council of Churches.

We are the more grateful for this visit, as we with our people know ourselves to be not only in a great company of suffering, but also in a solidarity of guilt. With great pain do we say: through us has endless suffering been brought to many peoples and countries. What we have often borne witness to in our own congregations, that we declare in the name of the whole Church. True, we have struggled for many years in the name of Jesus Christ against the spirit which has found its terrible expression in the National Socialist regime of violence, but we accuse ourselves for not being more courageous, for not praying more faithfully, for not believing more joyously and for not loving more ardently.

Now a new beginning is to be made in our Churches; founded on the Holy Scriptures, directed with all earnestness on the only Lord of the Church, they now proceed to cleanse themselves from influences alien to the faith and to set themselves in order. Our hope is in the God of grace and mercy, that He will use our churches as His instruments and will give them authority to proclaim His word, and in obedience to His will to work creatively among ourselves and among our whole people.

That in this new beginning we may become whole-heartedly united with other Churches of the Ecumenical Movement, fills us with deep joy.

We hope in God that through the common service of the Churches, the spirit of violence and revenge which again today wishes to become powerful may be brought under control in the whole world and the spirit of peace and love may gain the mastery, wherein alone tortured humanity can find healing.

So in an hour in which the whole world needs a new beginning, we pray VENI CREATOR SPIRITUS.

It was a brave utterance, and as one of the Frenchmen, Pierre Maury, said, 'it was not easy for you to make'. Thus was the way made plain for full participation of the German Church in the World Council.

Preparing for Amsterdam

The meeting of the Provisional Committee at Geneva was a landmark in the development of the World Council of Churches. Pastor Boegner presided. Some fifty representative churchmen from different parts of the world were present. The General Secretary gave a vivid account of the activities of the staff, and outlined the task of the World Council as he saw it in the coming years. He noted that the World Council had had a remarkable vote of confidence from the Churches. In spite of the utter uncertainty of the world situation, no fewer than fifty Churches had decided to join the Council since the summer of 1939, and had thus declared that they had confidence that the World Council would weather the storm. The Committee decided that the First Assembly should be held in 1948; that the main theme should be 'The Order of God and the present Disorder of Man'; and that in working out the detailed programme care should be taken by the Study Department to keep in close touch with the Churches.

All present realized the grave problem which the war and its aftermath raised. Special attention was paid to the desperate situation of millions of refugees and displaced persons, and the great hardship, distress, and suffering brought to millions through the transfers of population resulting from the Potsdam Conference. An appeal was made to the Allied Governments in the United Nations Organization for adequate provision for relief, and for an appropriate settlement of all the transferred populations in their new homes. In the words of the Message issued at the end of the meeting:

We therefore appeal especially to the Governments of the Five Great Powers to rise to their responsibilities to the world. It was by the union of their forces that they won the victory in the war. We ask them to unite their whole strength in a common purpose now for the establishment of justice, for the relief of hunger, and for the development of a world community of free peoples. Unless they turn from their old ways of reliance upon mere might and own their subjection to God's law of righteousness and love, they pursue the way of disaster and death.

Wednesday, 20 February, was a day of special significance for the ecumenical movement, for on that day the delegates of the International Missionary Council and of the World Council of Churches met together for an 'Ecumenical Consultation' during which, through reports from many Churches, the story of the Church of Christ during the years of struggle unfolded itself. In the afternoon the delegates were welcomed by the Swiss Churches and the Swiss Government. In the evening an unforgettable ecumenical service was held in the Protestant Cathedral, in which the Moderator of the Church of Geneva, the Archbishop of Canterbury, Archbishop Germanos, and the President of the Swiss Federation of Churches participated, while addresses were given by Dr Chester Miao (China), Bishop Berggrav, and Dr Martin Niemöller.

Preparations for the Assembly were carried a stage further when the Provisional Committee met again at Buck Hill Falls, Pennsylvania, in April 1947. By that time an invitation to the Assembly to meet in Amsterdam had been accepted. The question of the representation of the younger Churches, especially those in Asia and Africa, was considered, in close association with the International Missionary Council. A report of a delegation appointed to visit the Orthodox Churches to secure their co-operation was received. The delegation reported that the Provisional Committee 'can count upon the reaffirmed co-operation of the Churches which we visited and their full participation in the Assembly of 1948'.

Provision had also to be made for the finance required for so large an undertaking, including administration, travel of delegates, publicity, radio, publications of various kinds, etc. The responsibility for this was undertaken by Dr Henry Smith Leiper, Secretary of the 'Friends of the World Council of Churches' in U.S.A. He accomplished the task with outstanding success. Through appropriations from nineteen denominations, gifts from a large number of local congregations and individual benefactors, collections at ecumenical services, and special gifts, the total sum raised was 129,682 dollars. This is another example of the generosity of American churchmen; and also of Dr Leiper's ability, energy, powers of persuasion and unceasing devotion to the ecumenical cause over a great number of years.

Meanwhile the fact which dominated the situation of the World Council in 1947 was that its tasks and responsibilities had expanded in a way quite unforeseen in 1937, or even in 1945 and 1946. Four new Departments had been added in the past twelve months. The total income for all activities, which a few years ago was no more than 25,000 dollars, had gone up to millions. Growth had not been promoted by artificial means, but, as Dr Visser 't Hooft wrote, 'rather forced upon us by the realities of the situation'. 'This means,' he said, 'at least that the Council is truly needed. If it did not exist, it would have to be created. It performs tasks which must be performed in the name of the Church of Christ as a whole and which could not possibly be performed to the same extent and on the same level, if the Churches acted separately.'

5

THE WORLD COUNCIL STARTS:
AMSTERDAM, 1948

ON SUNDAY, 22 August 1948, at 3 p.m. the delegates of 147 Churches assembled for the opening session of the First Assembly of the World Council in the Nieuwe Kerk, Amsterdam. It was a thrilling moment, for here at last the hopes and prayers of years were to be fulfilled. Some of the oldest Churches in the world were represented – the Church of Ethiopia and the Orthodox Syrian Church of Malabar, for example; and some of the youngest, like the Presbyterian Church in Korea. Well-known leaders of the principal Churches in the United States and Canada were side by side with leaders of the Lutheran and Reformed Churches in different countries of Europe. Bishops of the Orthodox Church, the Anglican, and Old Catholic Churches, leaders of the Church of Scotland, and of the Evangelical Free Churches in Britain, with their colleagues in every continent, were there. Almost every grade of denomination was to be found: and more striking still, lay men and women and ministers of every colour and race. It was a truly international and inter-racial gathering, ecumenical in the largest sense; and all had come together as belonging to a fellowship of Churches which acknowledge our Lord Jesus Christ as God and Saviour.

The service itself was symbolic, not only in the presence of the various participants, or the diversity of the hymns and prayers from different sources, but also in the relation of the chief emblem of the Christian faith to the chief officiating minister, Dr Gravemeyer, of the Dutch Reformed Church;

for above the minister, as he led the worship at a reading desk in front of the gilded choir screen, gleamed the Crown of Royalty, surmounted by the Orb and the Cross of the universal Kingship of Christ. The preacher was the Reverend D. T. Niles (the present Evangelistic Secretary of the World Council), a Sinhalese Tamil Methodist.

It was the prelude to the acceptance of the Constitution of the World Council on the following day by the official delegates, in the main hall of the Concertgebouw. The effective resolution was carried without a dissentient vote. The World Council, which had been for so long in process of formation, was now formed. The Archbishop of Canterbury, who was chairman for the occasion, asked all to stand in silent prayer, and invoked God's blessing on the solemn decision.

The Roman Catholic Church was not represented; and the Russian Orthodox Church had declined to take part. But there were representatives of Churches in Eastern Europe, to make it clear that this was no Western Council; and there was a notable representation of the younger Churches of Asia and Africa.

It is hardly possible to convey in cold print the extraordinary depth of the impression made by the experience of Amsterdam on Church men and women from all over the world. The Assembly met in a beautiful city, and the delegates were received with abounding hospitality by the Churches of Holland, at a moment of great national rejoicing in the Netherlands. It was the Jubilee of Queen Wilhelmina. The investiture of her daughter as successor was about to take place; and the gratitude of the population to the sovereign who had ruled them so well for so long was soon to find its own expression in a series of jubilant demonstrations. The town was decorated by day, and illuminated by night. It gave the impression of festivity and enthusiasm. It was a town in which the main means of motion seemed to be by canal and bicycle. Certainly the latter thronged the streets in great quantities, ridden at a speed which sometimes caused not only admiration but alarm! Yet in spite of their impending national celebrations, the people of Amsterdam welcomed the 'ecumenists' of many races, and in diverse robes, in no uncertain fashion. There was official and unofficial hospitality from Palace and Government, from Church and City, and many were the expressions of gratitude to our hosts and the local Committee under the chairmanship of Dr Berkelbach van der Sprenkel.

Arrangements for religious worship were extremely good. Every day there were prayers, representing different ranges of liturgical expression, in the Koepelkerk. There were celebrations of the Holy Communion according to different rites, and following the rules of the different Churches responsible. On Sunday, 29 August, a great service of Holy Communion took place in the Nieuwe Kerk, at which the Reformed Church of Holland invited all baptized and communicant members of other Churches to participate. Some twelve hundred of those attending the Assembly took part. Ten ministers from different countries and different confessions sat in turn at the Communion Table, and spoke the words of Institution as each group of communicants came forward. The communicants moved towards the Table in groups of a hundred at a time. Members of the Orthodox Church were present, though they did not communicate; and others were present in a similar way. It was a most vivid and moving service for all who were there, as they listened to the sermon, sang the hymns, followed the liturgy, and took their various parts in the whole.

There was much business to be done by the Assembly: the framing of rules and regulations, laying down lines of policy, providing for finance, and dealing with certain concerns of the Churches, such as, in particular, the life and work of women in the Church, the significance of the laity, and the Christian approach to the Jews.

Man's Disorder and God's Design

There was one general theme by which all the other subjects for discussion were governed – 'Man's Disorder and God's Design'. But there were four particular subjects which fell under this general title: I. The Universal Church in God's Design. II. The Church's Witness to God's Design. III. The Church and the Disorder of Society. IV. The Church and the International Disorder. An immense amount of preparatory work had been done by means of correspondence, meetings of groups, circulation and revision of papers (some of which were later published in four volumes).

The proceedings began with a number of plenary sessions. Then the four subjects were allocated to four sections, between which the whole membership of the Assembly was distributed. The sections met every morning for six days, and then presented their reports to plenary sessions. The hardest and most exacting work of the Assembly was done in the sectional meetings. It was there that the debate was most eager, that deep convictions were best expressed, that the clash of minds took place, and that agreements and disagreements were formulated and recorded, on such issues, for example, as the meaning of Catholic and Protestant; the conflict between Capitalism and Communism; the question whether or not there is such a thing as a 'just war'.

In the plenary sessions certain moments stand out. No one who was present on the first Monday afternoon, 23 August, will forget the prophetic warnings and grave eloquence of Professor Karl Barth of Basel, and the way in which he pointed out the danger of all our counsels coming to naught unless we keep first things first: *first* God's Design, which is His and not ours, and must never be confused with any sort of 'Christian Marshall Plan' that we may concoct. 'Should we not come to the clear understanding,' he asked, 'that by "God's Design" is really meant His plan; that is, His already present, victorious, already founded Kingdom in all its majesty – our Lord Jesus Christ, who has already robbed sin and death, the devil and hell of their power, and already vindicated Divine and human justice in His own person?'

East and West

Another moment was that in which John Foster Dulles (U.S.A.) and Professor Josef Hromadka (Czechoslovakia) followed one another on the platform, with Dr John R. Mott as chairman. Here the West confronted the East in a vivid way, and the effect on the audience was electrical. The international situation was full of anxieties. No one knew what might happen in the next few weeks. Mr Dulles began by remarking that this illustration of unity came at a fateful hour. The Assembly showed a unity in diversity which was of the kind needed to save mankind from disaster. War might be the lesser of two evils: but there is no holy war, and there is no reason to think that a new war would accomplish any good. Having said that, he spoke vigorously of the principles and virtues of Western democracy at some length.

Professor Hromadka followed with a challenge. The Church had no illusions, he said, about man and the world. No gold, or silk, or iron curtains must separate Christians. But, he said, we are witnessing the end of Western supremacy. Henceforth the West must share world responsibility with the East. It must get over its horror of new world trends and Russia. Many barbarians are through the Communist movement coming of age, and aspiring to a place in the sun. The Church must lend its sympathy to these new barbarians.

Two fine expositions were given, one on the Churches' Witness to the World, by Bishop Stephen Neill, and the other by Mrs Kathleen Bliss, on the Church's need of understanding modern, scientific, technical society, and on the tragic division within the Church between clergy and laity – as well as the division between Church and world.

Among the public unofficial meetings was one at which Martin Niemöller made an extraordinary impression upon the youth of Amsterdam. Knowing the record of the German occupation, Niemöller was apprehensive as to the reception he was likely to get. The meeting was crowded. The Dutch layman who presided introduced him as one who belonged to a country from which Holland had suffered deeply, and who had suffered deeply himself for his convictions. He was received with immense applause, the whole meeting rising to its feet with ringing cheers.

As the delegates looked up at the platform in the Concertgebouw from the body of the hall, they saw what looked like telephone boxes, with glass doors, in which the interpreters were immured, translating all the speeches as delivered simultaneously into the different languages with great skill. Occasionally they were completely defeated, as when Dr Reinhold Niebuhr, speaking with an eloquence and at a pace remarkable even for him, caused them to throw down their earphones in despair! Delegates looking up at the platform would also see the bright concourse of 100 youth delegates, following the proceedings with rapt attention. These had their own separate sections, like the official delegates, and their alternates, when they considered the problems of the Church, Evangelism, the Responsible Society, and War. They did their part with great ability, and won a burst of applause at the end of the session when Philip Potter, a West Indian from Jamaica, presented a statement on behalf of his colleagues with both charm and force.

We intend to stay together

Amongst the moments most likely to remain in the memories of the delegates was the moment when the Message was presented and, after criticism, approved. It was hard to know what kind of Message would both do justice to the general sense of what the delegates had in their minds, and also satisfy criticisms as to the manner of expression, with neither too little nor too much of the apocalyptic fervour. The preparation of it was entrusted to a Message Committee of twenty-one, an admirable company including some of the best minds of the Assembly from East and West. They knew that the Assembly wanted to express the gratitude of the Churches to God for bringing them together. They knew too that they wanted to remain together. They knew that God had something to say through the Assembly to the world. Various drafts were submitted from various quarters. In the end, however, it was a draft conflated by a young Bishop of the Church of South India, Lesslie Newbigin, who was not a member of the Committee at all but had the ardour and the gift for expressing the mind of the Assembly, which enabled the various members of the Message Committee to come together on a common ground. The Message consists of 1,000 words: but the section which remains in the memory of all is this: 'Here at Amsterdam we have committed ourselves afresh to Him, and have covenanted with one another in constituting this World Council of Churches. We intend to stay together.'

6

THE ORTHODOX CHURCHES AND
THE ABSENCE OF RUSSIA

EIGHTY-FIVE places (out of a total of 450) had been provisionally set aside for the Orthodox Churches throughout
the world, to be allocated by them in such manner as they
might decide. The Church of Greece was officially represented at the Assembly. Archbishop Germanos of Thyateïra,
one of the Joint Presidents of the World Council, was
the leader of an influential delegation from the Ecumenical Patriarchate of Constantinople. Members of certain
other Orthodox Churches were also present. But although,
as Dr Visser 't Hooft explained to the Assembly, the Provisional Committee had made it as clear as possible to the
Orthodox Church of Russia that its full participation would
be welcome, that great Church declined to send either delegates or observers. Nor were there any delegates from the
Orthodox Churches in the countries most closely attached
to the U.S.S.R.

The full participation of the Orthodox Churches is a
matter of great moment to the World Council of Churches.
On no account ought the World Council to be allowed to
give the impression of being either an organization of Protestant Churches, or largely a Western, and, more specifically, an Anglo-Saxon organization, which identifies itself,
consciously or unconsciously, with the concerns and interests
of Western nations. As Dr Visser 't Hooft told the Provisional Committee at its meeting in the United States in
1947, the World Council would lose its *raison d'être* if it did
not attempt to establish a deep and permanent contact

between the Churches of the West and those of the East. 'The Eastern Churches have maintained a sense of the objective reality and the cosmic dimensions of the drama of salvation which the Western Churches need to recapture. They are today going through a crisis which may well prove a crisis into life and in which they must be able to count on the fraternal sympathy and help of their sister-Churches of other confessions.'

Orthodox Appeal for League of Churches

From 1920 onwards the Orthodox Churches have given evidence of their concern with and interest in the ecumenical movement. The delegation from the Protestant Episcopal Church in the United States which visited Europe at the end of the First World War, to promote a world conference of the Churches on Faith and Order, received a most cordial welcome at the Ecumenical Patriarchate, and from the Bishops of Orthodox Churches in the Balkans. In January 1920 the Ecumenical Patriarchate issued an Encyclical Letter appealing to all the Churches of Christ for closer intercourse and mutual understanding. The timing of this Encyclical was most significant. At the very moment when the whole Christian population of Asia Minor, 1,500,000 Greek Orthodox whose ancestors had lived there as Christians ever since S. Paul brought the Gospel, were being ruthlessly expelled, this wonderful call rang out from the heart of Orthodoxy. It was an appeal for the formation of 'a League of Churches to promote Christian unity and solidarity against the growing power of anti-Christ which menaces the whole Hellenic Christian civilization'.

A delegation of eighteen Orthodox churchmen from seven Eastern Churches came to Geneva for the preparatory conference of the Faith and Order movement in August 1920. This was an important moment in the development of the whole ecumenical movement, and the early identification of the Orthodox Church with the movement at this stage was a substantial evidence of its sympathy and interest. Three of the delegates also attended the preparatory meeting for the Life and Work movement held at the same place. It was as a result of these meetings in Geneva that the Orthodox Churches outside Russia came into the ecumenical movement; and from the conferences of Stockholm and Lausanne onwards their representatives have taken an active part in the Continuation Committees, and commissions of various sorts to which they have led. Professor Hamilcar Alivisatos of Athens, and Professor Stephan Zankow of Sofia, have been two of the most eager champions of ecumenical study and intercourse amongst the theologians and scholars of the Orthodox Churches in Greece, Rumania, Yugoslavia, and Bulgaria, and the Russian emigration. No one could have done more than each of them has done unremittingly and with ardour, from the very start in their respective ways, for the whole ecumenical movement.

Orthodox and Protestant

But it has to be recognized that the great majority of the member Churches in the World Council are Protestant Churches; and the very different conceptions of the Christian faith within those Churches do create great difficulties for the Orthodox Church, with its common tradition. This fact makes even discussion with Protestant Churches — much more agreement — difficult. There are differences, for example, in their attitudes to the Bible. The Orthodox Church, like all other Churches, fully recognizes the authority of the Bible; but it feels a responsibility for the right interpretation of the Bible. The Orthodox are indeed inclined to believe that the many divisions of Protestantism are chiefly due to the lack of an established tradition in the interpretation of the Bible. Another great difference lies in the conception of the nature of the Church. Protestants usually regard the Church as the congregation of all true believers in Christ. Orthodox would accept this as right in principle, but as an inadequate definition, for they insist on stressing the organic, ecclesiastical and institutional order of the visible Church as constituted by our Lord and the Apostles. Further, for the Orthodox Church love is so intimately bound up with faith that justification by faith alone, regarded quite absolutely, is difficult to understand. In the liturgy of the Greek Church, love is preliminary to confession. 'Let us love one another in order that we may confess,' says the deacon just before the creed. Again, there are wide divergences in the attitude of the Protestant Churches and the Orthodox Church to the Eucharist; the Orthodox doctrine of the *metabole*, or mysterious change in the elements being very different from the Roman doctrine of transubstantiation, or the denial by many Protestants of any change or any special presence of Christ. Further, while Protestantism stresses the individual soul, Orthodoxy, while valuing the individual, never loses sight of the fact that the Christian liberty of the soul exists within the community and fellowship of the Church.

But in spite of these serious doctrinal differences, especially in the conception of the nature of the Church and worship, and of the means of grace, not only an understanding but a closer contact between these two great Christian traditions is entirely possible. Indeed such a close co-operation has been in large measure achieved during the last forty years, by means of the ecumenical movement.

I say all this with full confidence, after discussion with Orthodox friends for many years, both before and since the Second World War. And I have been much helped for my present purpose by advice, both in conversation and in writing (some of which I have quoted above) from

Professor Hamilcar Alivisatos, the great theologian of Athens.

Difficult Situation of Orthodox Churches

The Orthodox Churches are at present separated from one another by political conditions. The hope so often entertained of a pan-Orthodox conference, at which matters of common interest to all Orthodox Churches, including their relation to the World Council of Churches, could be discussed, has not yet been realized, and the prospects of such a conference in the near future do not look promising. This fact in itself makes the expression of a united Orthodox judgement on the World Council at present impossible. Up to now the several Orthodox Churches have come to ecumenical conferences as separate Churches. They have been invited one by one to take part in the conferences, and have sent strong delegations – with the great exception of the Russian Orthodox Church, which has been so specially isolated ever since the Revolution of 1917. Some of the Orthodox representatives were amongst the most regular and eager at ecumenical meetings before the Second World War – such men as Bishop Iriney of Yugoslavia, Archbishop Stefan and Professor Zankow of Bulgaria. They are now no longer able to take part; but the debt of the ecumenical movement to them is immense, and the hope of contact with the Churches which they adorn remains unwavering. Contributions of great value from the Orthodox side continue to be made, for example by theologians of the Russian emigration, notably Professor Florovsky: and outstanding in its firm adherence to the ecumenical movement is the great Orthodox Church of the Patriarchate of Constantinople, with Archbishop Athenagoras taking the place of Archbishop Germanos.

For the reasons given it follows that the actual representation of Orthodoxy able to attend ecumenical meetings forms a very small minority in comparison with the great majority of Protestants, though there are special links between the Orthodox and the Anglicans and Old Catholics. And yet though they are few in number, they represent in spirit and quality the whole Orthodox world. Their actual contribution at ecumenical gatherings is precious, their potential contribution in years to come impossible to calculate. And it should never be forgotten by the great bulk of Christians in all the member Churches that it is just because of their care for tradition, their organic doctrine of the Church and the Sacraments, their stability, their emphasis on love, and their sufferings, that they form a factor in the World Council of Churches which is essential to the Council's service to truth, justice, and charity.

Archbishop Germanos

It is no exaggeration to say that the contribution which the Orthodox Churches have made and are making to the whole ecumenical movement is unique and indispensable. Nor would any account either of the Orthodox contribution or of the ecumenical movement be complete without paying a special tribute to their great spokesman and leader, Archbishop Germanos of Thyateira. As Dean of the Faculty of Theology of Chalki at Constantinople, he took part in the first Faith and Order meeting at Geneva in 1920. From the time of the Stockholm Conference in 1925 onwards he was the most unfailing and outstanding representative of the Orthodox Churches in both the Faith and Order and the Life and Work movements. He was devoted to the ecumenical ideal, and both a courteous interpreter of the Orthodox Churches to other Churches, and a wise and considerate expounder of the ecumenical movement to his brethren in the Orthodox Churches. He died in London in January

1951, at the age of 83, leaving a memory which will remain as a constant inspiration for many years to come.

The Church of Russia

The Church of Russia has been missing from all the delegations representing the Orthodox Churches. For the larger part of these thirty years there has been all too little contact between other countries and Russia, and as a result between the Russian Church and other Churches. But at the end of the Second World War the Provisional Committee determined to do what it could to establish a relationship with the Patriarchate of Moscow.

At the first meeting of the Provisional Committee after the war, at Geneva in February 1946, a resolution was passed authorizing its officials and the Administrative Committee to take steps to make a special approach both to the Greek-speaking Churches and to the Church of Russia. The approach to the Church of Russia was made by a direct invitation to the Patriarch to send a delegation to meet a delegation of representatives of the World Council, in Prague or elsewhere, to discuss the whole question of participation in the World Council. The Patriarch accepted the invitation, and an agreement was reached both as to the time and the place of the meeting at the end of 1947. But the meeting did not take place, as the Patriarch of Moscow did not consider that the Patriarchate was sufficiently prepared for it. Correspondence however continued. On 29 March 1948 the Patriarch wrote to the General Secretary, 'Permit me to thank the World Council in your person for its kind invitation to the Russian Church to participate in the ecumenical movement. We would like to act on your request, and to give an answer to this invitation not later than the month of April'.

Nothing more was heard, however, till the holding of a

Conference at Moscow of heads and representatives of Autocephalous Orthodox Churches, 8–10 July 1948, in connexion
with the celebration of 500 years of autocephalicity of the
Russian Orthodox Church. The other Churches represented
were the Churches of Constantinople, Antioch, Alexandria,
Georgia, Serbia, Rumania, Bulgaria, Greece, Albania, and
Poland, with representatives of the Moscow Patriarchate
from other countries, and the Armenian Patriarch. It had a
comprehensive agenda, including: The Orthodox Church
and the Papacy; The Validity of Anglican Ordinations;
The Church Calendar; The Ecumenical Movement and the
Orthodox Church. A report on the ecumenical movement
had been prepared beforehand by a Russian writer who had
no personal knowledge of that movement, with the result that
it gave an entirely misleading account and created a quite
false impression of it and its work. Addresses were given
from different angles about the movement. But those taking
part in the discussion had had no first-hand experience of
the movement, with the result that its method and purpose
were woefully misunderstood. A few lonely voices which
sought to explain its true character were not heard. A
Resolution was adopted by the Conference, of which the
conclusion is as follows:

Taking account of this present situation, our Conference of heads
and representatives of Autocephalous Orthodox Churches, having
prayerfully invoked the presence of the Holy Spirit, has decided:
To inform the 'World Council of Churches', in reply to the
invitation we have all received to participate in the Amsterdam
Assembly as members, that all the national Orthodox Churches
taking part in the present Conference are obliged to decline participation in the ecumenical movement, in its present form.

The arguments leading up to this decision were reflected
in the preamble. Thus (a) it describes the purpose of the
ecumenical movement 'expressed in the formation of the
World Council of Churches, with its consequent aim of

organizing an "Ecumenical Church"' as 'not in accord with the ideals of Christianity and the aims of the Church of Christ as they are understood by the Orthodox Church'. (*b*) It speaks of its 'effort by means of social and political activity for the creation of an Ecumenical Church as an international influence'. (*c*) It states that the ecumenical movement in its present scheme has too early lost faith in the possibility of union in one Holy, Catholic, and Apostolic Church. (*d*) It regrets that from 1937 to 1948 there has been no further discussion on the idea of union of the Churches on dogmatic and confessional grounds. Lastly (*e*) it criticizes 'the reduction of requirements and conditions for unity to the simple recognition of Christ as Our Lord'.

There are many complete misconceptions in these reflections and arguments; and an extraordinary failure to take account of the continuous and systematic work for reunion, based on Faith and Order, to which Orthodox scholars have contributed, during the whole of this period. In sending a copy of the resolution to the General Secretary on 1 August 1948, the Metropolitan Nikolai, after describing the circumstances of the Conference, and also dissociating the Russian Church from any participation by other Russians, even though they may be Russian by nationality and Orthodox by confession, ends his letter thus:

However, this refusal on our part does not mean that we shall not be interested in the activities of the Ecumenical Movement. The Russian Orthodox Church, besides, has not lost confidence in the possibility of reunion in grace with her, by God's help, of any Christian confession or body. She is ready to have direct connexion with them with the object of their reunion, without running to the World Council of Churches as intermediary.

In view of this, we would ask you to continue to keep us informed regarding the activities of the World Council of Churches, sending to us suitable literature, reports on the assemblies and conferences, papers on all questions, and so forth.

It was certainly a disappointment that there had been no

opportunity of personal discussion between representatives of the Russian Orthodox Church and representatives of the World Council of Churches before the Moscow Conference was held; and that there has been no opportunity of such a discussion since Amsterdam. Literature and documents have been continuously sent by the World Council to the Russian Patriarchate, and it is to be hoped that opportunities for full personal discussion may yet be given in the not too distant future.

7

THE REFUSAL OF ROME

THE Roman Catholic Church believes that it alone is the One Holy, Catholic, and Apostolic Church founded by Jesus Christ and witnessed to in the Creeds. The necessity of the papal supremacy for the true life of the Church lies in the fact that 'Christ, the Head of the Body' rules the Church, not only by 'invisible and extraordinary government', but also by 'visible and ordinary government, in the Universal Church through the Roman Pontiff'. Christ is the principal Head of the Church, but rules the Church on earth through his Vicar, and if this visible Head is eliminated 'and the visible bonds of unity broken, the mystical Body of the Redeemer is so obscured and disfigured that it becomes impossible for those who are seeking the harbour of eternal salvation to see or discover it'. This doctrine is clearly laid down in the Encyclicals of Pope Pius XII, *Mystici Corporis Christi* (1943), and *Humani Generis* (1950). The Roman Catholic Church teaches that the only way by which Christian unity can be achieved is for the separated brethren to draw nigh to the Apostolic See, and submit themselves to its teaching and government. It is only on the basis that the Roman Catholic Church stands unalterably by this belief and teaching that there can be any fruitful discussion of the relationship of that Church to other Churches.

Some separated groups of Christians in Eastern Christendom have been persuaded to leave their ancient Orthodox allegiance and submit to the Pope. When they have submitted, they have often been allowed to retain their old traditions and customs, their liturgy, for example, and a married clergy, but always at the price of accepting the supremacy of the Pope, and abandoning the 'heresies' to which they were committed. But their very submission has made the whole Orthodox Church not only most unwilling to treat with Rome about union, but also very insistent in their outcry against proselytism.

This belief and teaching govern Rome's relationships alike with individual Churches, and with the ecumenical movement. The ecumenical movement is however a movement which seeks to express a relationship between Churches which accept our Lord Jesus Christ as God and Saviour. Even though many Orthodox and Protestant churchmen might look askance at particular features in the Church of Rome, ought not an approach to be made to the authorities of that Church (it has been asked), with a view to some means of association being found between it and them?

Early Approaches Rebuffed

Successive attempts were accordingly made by the early leaders. Archbishop Söderblom sought unsuccessfully to enlist the interest of Rome in the Stockholm Conference on Life and Work in 1925. An attempt was also made, with a similar lack of success, to secure some sort of participation of the Roman Catholic Church, however informally, in the Lausanne Conference on Faith and Order in 1927. But the Roman Catholic Church did not simply refuse to participate. It attacked. On 6 January 1928, Pope Pius XI issued the Encyclical *Mortalium Animos* which was quite uncompromising in its condemnation of the ecumenical movement as a whole. It declared that 'these pan-Christians who strive for the union of the Churches would appear to pursue the noblest of ideals in promoting charity among all Christians. But how should charity tend to the detriment of faith?' It went on to say that 'since the foundation of charity is faith pure and inviolate, it is chiefly by the bond of one faith that the disciples of Christ are to be united. A federation of Christians, then, is inconceivable in which each member retains his own opinions and private judgement in matters of faith, even though they differ from the opinions of all the rest'. It concluded that 'there is but one way in which the unity of Christians may be fostered, and that is by furthering the return to the one true Church of Christ of those who are separated from it; for from that one true Church they have in the past fallen away. The one Church of Christ is visible to all, and will remain, according to the will of its Author, exactly the same as He instituted it'. It was not surprising that Archbishop Söderblom should repudiate in strong terms what he asserted to be a caricature of the ecumenical movement; and the total failure of the Encyclical both to distinguish between faith as intellectual assent and faith as the trustful submission of the soul to God, and to establish correctly the relationship between faith and love.

Meanwhile active discussions were taking place among many Roman Catholic scholars who were deeply impressed by the fact and the range of the ecumenical movement. This was notably the case in Belgium and France. Fr Congar and his circle, and the Benedictine monks of Amay may be specially mentioned. So it came about that many personal contacts were made between Roman Catholic thinkers and thinkers of other Churches.

No Roman Catholic delegates attended the Oxford Conference of 1937. But at Edinburgh the Roman Catholic Archbishop of Edinburgh allowed four priests and one layman to come as unofficial observers. The Oxford and Edinburgh Conferences both passed resolutions approving the formation of a World Council of Churches. Accordingly in February 1939 Archbishop Temple (Chairman of the Provisional Committee) as an act of courtesy informed the Holy See that the World Council was being established. He was in turn informed by the Cardinal Secretary of State, through the Apostolic Delegate to Great Britain, that, while the Roman Church was not desirous of formally associating itself with the World Council, there was no obstacle in the way of consultation with the Bishops and the Apostolic Delegate, or of an exchange of confidential information with Catholic theologians.

The Question of Observers at Amsterdam

Although no further communications took place with the Vatican, there were a large number of informal and personal contacts between some of those closely connected with the Provisional Committee of the World Council and Roman Catholic theologians; and when the Provisional Committee held its first post-war meeting at Geneva in February 1946, Bishop Charrière, Roman Catholic Bishop of Lausanne, Geneva, and Fribourg, sent a very friendly letter to Bishop Brilioth (Sweden), one of its members.

In April 1947 the Provisional Committee decided that a few individual Roman Catholics should be invited to attend the Assembly as 'unofficial observers'. A considerable number of letters reached the General Secretary from Roman Catholic priests and laymen, asking to be invited. Additional names were proposed by World Council leaders; and from one unofficial Roman Catholic source a list was received with fourteen names of Roman Catholics who had made a special study of ecumenical questions. This list included the names of persons who (like some of the applicants previously mentioned) had the full support of their Bishop or superior in their desire to attend the Amsterdam Assembly. All these names were considered, and in the first months of 1948 some ten persons were invited.

An intimation then arrived from or on behalf of Cardinal de Jong, Archbishop of Utrecht, that he considered that the choice of observers should be approved by the Roman

Catholic Hierarchy of the Netherlands. All those, therefore, who had been invited were informed by the General Secretary of this fact, with a view to each taking whatever action he considered to be right. The General Secretary also let the Roman Catholic authorities of the Netherlands know that if they desired to propose names, these would be considered along with the names already received. But no further names were received from Cardinal de Jong.

On 5 June the Holy Office issued the Monitum *Cum compertum*, according to which laymen or priests were reminded that it was forbidden to take part in ecumenical meetings without authorization from the Vatican. This official declaration coming at that late hour effectively closed the door to the participation by any Roman Catholic observers or visitors in the proceedings of the Assembly. No authorization from the Vatican was received by any of the Roman Catholics who had been in touch, directly or indirectly, with the General Secretary. Prayers were asked for the Assembly by means of a Pastoral Letter of the Roman Catholic Bishops in Holland, read in all Roman Catholic churches in the Netherlands on Sunday, 22 August. But the only Roman Catholic persons attending the Assembly were some journalists who represented the Roman Catholic press.

I have told the story of the leading factors behind the non-participation of Roman Catholics in the Assembly at Amsterdam. It must not however be assumed that all the Churches represented on the Provisional Committee readily agreed that Roman Catholic observers might be invited. The delegates of some Churches objected on the ground that the teaching of the Church of Rome was so contrary in important matters to the teaching of the Gospel that they were bound in conscience to express their opposition. The strongest objection was based on the ground of the denial of religious freedom to Protestants in Italy, Spain, and certain countries in South America, a denial in some cases

accompanied by physical violence. At the same time the
large majority of the representatives of the member Churches
desire that the way to co-operation with Rome to be
kept open, so that the fellowship of Christians might be
complete.

A New Instruction

No communication has passed between Geneva and the
Vatican since Amsterdam. But the Vatican itself, on 20
December 1949, issued an Instruction to Local Ordinaries
on the Ecumenical Movement. The interpretation of the
ecumenical movement contained in this Instruction is a very
limited one. It seems almost to identify it with 'the reconciliation of dissident Christians with the Catholic Church'.
But while it begins with the clear statement 'The Catholic
Church takes no part in "ecumenical" conferences or meetings', the Instruction does give a limited encouragement to
conferences between Roman Catholics and others, with the
proviso that they are under official control.

It is particularly stated that the Monitum of June 1948
does not apply 'to those mixed gatherings where Catholics
and non-Catholics meet, not to discuss matters of faith and
morals, but to take counsel together concerning joint action
in the defence of the fundamental principles of Christianity
and the natural law; nor does it apply to occasions when they
meet to deal with the rebuilding of the social order and
similar questions'.

Further, while very strict conditions are laid down as to
reports to the Bishop, and ultimately to the Vatican, recognition is given to inter-diocesan national and international
conferences, on which Catholics and non-Catholics meet,
subject to permission being obtained each time from the
Holy See. Moreover (and perhaps this is the most obvious
advance) 'it is not forbidden to open or close these gather-

ings with the common recitation of the Lord's Prayer or some other prayer approved by the Catholic Church'.

The provisions of this Instruction may not go very far. On the one hand it registers a definite advance towards co-operation since the time of the Stockholm Conference of 1925. On the other hand it requires a stricter control where co-operation is attempted. The question remains – Do Christians yet perceive that Catholicism, Protestantism, and Orthodoxy are threatened by a common enemy – materialism – far more formidable to each than each is to the other? Do Christians yet understand how vital it is that Catholicism, Protestantism, and Orthodoxy should find a way to a closer association in matters outside the dogmatic field for a common witness to the Kingship of Christ?

8

HOW THE WORLD COUNCIL WORKS

THE World Council has a Basis, which Churches applying for membership accept. It is not a credal test to judge Churches or persons. It is an affirmation of the Incarnation and Atonement. The first Article in the Constitution accordingly reads as follows: 'The World Council of Churches is a fellowship of churches which accept our Lord Jesus Christ as God and Saviour. It is constituted for the discharge of the functions set out below.' The second Article explains that Churches which express their agreement with this Basis, and satisfy such criteria as the Assembly or the Central Committee may prescribe (particularly autonomy, stability, size, and relationship with other Churches) are eligible for membership, election being by a two-thirds vote of the member Churches. The third Article sets forth the functions:

  (i) To carry on the work of the two world movements for Faith and Order and for Life and Work.

 (ii) To facilitate common action by the Churches.

(iii) To promote co-operation in study.

 (iv) To promote the growth of ecumenical consciousness in the members of all Churches.

  (v) To establish relations with denominational federations of world-wide scope and with other ecumenical movements.

 (vi) To call world conferences on specific subjects as occasion may require, such conferences being empowered to publish their own findings.

(vii) To support the Churches in their task of evangelism.

Organization and Finance

On the side of organization the World Council discharges its functions through (1) an Assembly, which is the principal authority, and ordinarily meets every five years. It is composed of official representatives, clerical and lay, of the Churches, the number of members being determined by the preceding Assembly. (2) A Central Committee, consisting of a President or Presidents, and not more than ninety members chosen by the Assembly from among the persons whom the Churches have appointed as members of the Assembly. The Central Committee meets normally once every year, and exercises the functions of the Assembly in between Assembly meetings. It appoints its own Executive Committee.

The World Council also discharges part of its functions by the appointment of Commissions, consisting of clerical and lay persons, not limited to members of the Assembly: for example, the Commission on Faith and Order, and the Commission of the Churches on International Affairs. Great care has been taken in the Constitution to guard against any suggestion that the World Council should control or legislate for the Churches. It is 'to offer counsel and provide opportunity of united action in matters of common interest'. 'It may take action on behalf of constituent Churches in such matters as one or more of them may commit to it.' 'It disavows any thought of becoming a single unified Church structure independent of the Churches which have joined in constituting the Council, or a structure dominated by a centralized administrative authority.'

There are provisions in the Constitution for linking up the World Council with world confessional organizations, the International Missionary Council, and particular ecumenical organizations, such as the great world Youth movements.

There are at present five Presidents: Pastor Marc Boegner (France); the Archbishop of Canterbury (Dr Geoffrey

Fisher); Bishop G. Bromley Oxnam (U.S.A.); Archbishop Athenagoras of Thyateira; and Bishop Berggrav (Norway). There is one vacancy caused by the death of Miss Sarah Chakko (India) – a grievous loss to the whole ecumenical movement. Dr John R. Mott is an honorary President. The General Secretary is Dr W. A. Visser 't Hooft. There are also Associate General Secretaries, and Heads of Departments. The main office is at 17 Route de Malagnou, Geneva.

Finance

The finances of the World Council have been managed under the direction of a Finance Committee, of which Bishop Oxnam is Chairman. No organization could be better served by a Chairman of its Finance Committee than the World Council of Churches has been served by him. And anyone who has had anything to do with the financing of the Council's work during the past six years would agree that (in Bishop Oxnam's words) 'there has been no thought in the minds of those who have been called to give largely at the moment, that such giving should in any way mean unusual privilege or undue influence in policy'.

The budget in 1949 was 559,600 dollars, which included 196,600 dollars for the Inter-Church Aid Department. The budget for 1953 totalled 355,000 dollars; but this no longer includes Inter-Church Aid. The main part was revenue from member churches; 240,000 dollars being contributed from member Churches in the U.S.A., and 75,000 dollars from member Churches in other countries. The Churches represented on the British Council of Churches contributed £5,250 (almost one-fifth of 75,000 dollars.)

Work for Youth

The work of the Central Committee, and certain Commissions and Departments is described in later chapters. But since it will not be the subject of separate treatment, mention may be made here of the Youth Department, which was constituted by the Central Committee in 1948. Its special task is to secure that the youth of the Churches are brought into the life of the World Council at all levels. It is doing invaluable work in connexion with the youth departments of member Churches, and with youth organizations. It arranges youth conferences in different parts of the world; and had a large share in the arrangements for the Christian Youth Congress at Travancore in 1952. It provides for the exchange of information and experience between the Churches in the East and the West, and takes care to secure, so far as it can, that work such as Inter-Church Aid, Work Camps, Bible Study, Faith and Order, is brought within the reach or the understanding of young people in the member Churches. By her visits to different Churches and different parts of the world, including Asia, Miss Jean Fraser, Secretary of the Youth Department, is doing a very significant work in linking up youth leaders of many races, nations and Churches with one another.

Maintaining Fellowship

Leaving the question of organization on one side, there are certain general observations which may be usefully made. The World Council of Churches has amongst others two particular duties complementary to each other, of maintaining fellowship, and giving its witness to the Kingship of Christ. It is of its very essence that it is a fellowship of Churches. In other words, it is infinitely more than an organization. It is a fellowship built upon a common faith, and is precious to all the Churches belonging to it. But it is peculiarly precious to the Churches which are cut off from their neighbours, or are forced to struggle for their spiritual life. The very fact that the World Council is a fellowship of

Churches, a means of communication from Church to Church; and that it has a continuing life, with officers who can keep in personal touch with the Churches, not only by correspondence but also by paying visits, gives a sense of living and personal fellowship. It is also world-wide in its range. The members of the World Council are members of an ecumenical body, scattered throughout the world. 'Ecumenicity', writes Sir Alfred Zimmern, 'is or should be a much closer bond than internationalism. It is not a bond between two independent groups: it is membership in a single group.'[1] Thus the World Council is a fellowship of Churches diverse from one another, and living under diverse political, social, and economic conditions, but bound to one another in spite of political or social or economic, or other secular differences. It ought to be particularly on its guard against anything savouring of unfairness to any of the member Churches, or any lack of sympathy or understanding in reference to their concerns. It is a fellowship which binds together Churches in the East and the West, which have accepted the basis of membership; and should do everything it can to strengthen and deepen the reality of that fellowship.

Duty of Witness

But it also has the duty of witness. From time to time this living fellowship will find public expression in a common word. The very existence of the World Council, says Dr Visser 't Hooft, proclaims the good news that Jesus Christ unites men of all Churches, nations, and races. But that witness is incomplete if it does not lead on to a clear common proclamation of the Lordship of Christ in all realms of life. The demand that the Churches as gathered together in the World Council should speak out and take a clear stand in

1. *Spiritual Values and World Affairs*, p. 67.

relation to the idolatries, the crimes and temptations of our chaotic age, comes with all the more insistence now that a number of Churches have, after a very long period of silence, realized again that the Church has a prophetic ministry to perform. This insight must permeate the whole ecumenical Church. Such common testimony has an especial significance for minority Churches or for Churches suffering isolation. The world also needs to hear a clear united voice which confronts it with the reality of God's judgement and God's grace.

The finding of the common word now, however, is not a simple thing. The World Council has no common spiritual language. While Churches are at one in recognizing the authority of Holy Scripture, there are deep divergences between them as to the precise significance of that authority for the life of the Church. A common word must be untainted by particular political or secular ideologies. The witness must be a witness to the Word of God. All fear of the political or organizational or other all too human considerations must be expelled. The churchmen who are present at any particular meeting for the purpose of listening for God's voice and then speaking to the Church must have a strong sense of responsibility to the Churches they represent, and be prepared successfully to justify such a public statement to those Churches when they return.

From what has just been said it will be plain that the function of maintaining the fellowship, and the function of offering witness are complementary to one another. Both are essential, and a right balance has to be kept between them. The World Council is young. In the early stages special care has to be taken to strengthen the bonds which bind its members together. It has also to be remembered that it is a *World* Council, not a Council of Churches of the Western countries; and that the delegates from Churches in Eastern countries have a claim on the attention of the

Council which is all the stronger because of the empty places waiting to be filled by delegates from other Churches in Eastern Europe, who would be much more numerous and perhaps influential in debate. Special account must also be taken of the younger Churches, which have an importance out of proportion to their numerical strength. As one of the Indian delegates remarked, 'More than half the population of the earth lives in the lands of the younger Churches, and their delegates represent not only their particular Churches, but also the countries in which they live and the cultures in which they move'.

9

THE FIRST SIX YEARS:
1948–1954

WITHIN a few hours of the conclusion of the Assembly on 4 September 1948, the delegates of the Churches dispersed to their homes. They had shared an unforgettable experience. They had been brought together at Amsterdam. They were united in acknowledging Jesus Christ as God and Saviour. They had made a covenant with one another in constituting the World Council and they had declared 'We intend to stay together'.

One of the last acts of the Assembly was to elect Joint Presidents, and to appoint the ninety members of the Central Committee. This Committee, which includes the Joint Presidents *ex officio*, is the permanent Committee which is charged with carrying out the Assembly's instructions, and exercising its functions, except that of amending the Constitution, or modifying the allocation of its own members. It has to formulate the budget and secure financial support. It names and elects its own officers and appoints its own secretarial staff. It meets normally once every calendar year. It is obvious, therefore, that the responsibility of the Central Committee is great, and that on its conduct of the business of the World Council, and above all on the wisdom and ability of the officers whom it appoints, under God, the well-being of the Council depends.

In subsequent chapters I shall deal specifically with the particular activities of certain Departments of the Council which require ampler treatment. But the simplest way of interpreting the growth of the World Council during the years which have followed Amsterdam is through an account of the meetings and actions of the Central Committee.

The task of the Central Committee

The first meeting was held at Woudschoeten, in Holland, immediately after the Assembly. Since that date it has met in successive years, for a week at a time, at Chichester (England), Toronto (Canada), Rolle (Switzerland), and Lucknow (India). The membership is comprehensive, including lay men and women, and takes due account both of adequate confessional representation and adequate geographical distribution. At Woudschoeten I received the great honour of being elected Chairman; and Dr Franklin Clark Fry, President of the United Lutheran Church in America, was similarly elected Vice-Chairman. About two-thirds of the members were new to the ecumenical movement, and were for the most part strangers to one another before Amsterdam. But one of the most encouraging features of the meetings has been the large and regular attendance. The result has been that members have come to know one another more and more intimately, and to appreciate the different points of view of the Churches and countries from which their colleagues come. There has been a great readiness to listen, and complete freedom for the expression of differences of conviction. All this has been greatly assisted by the arrangements for worship during the meetings, and by the warm hospitality which the members have received from their hosts, as well as by the preparation of material, and previous planning by the Executive Committee and the staff. The Central Committee between 1948 and 1954 has become a strong, cohesive body of Christian brethren, nearly all of them men and women holding posts of responsibility in their own Churches.

The agenda of the Central Committee always includes

general business, reports of the General Secretary and the Executive Committee, two or three Main Themes, and the reports of the Departments. The report of the General Secretary is one of the most important items. In it Dr Visser 't Hooft gives a wide and illuminating survey of some of the principal issues, as he sees them, in the ecumenical movement during the previous twelve months, and of reactions and counter-currents, as well as describing his own experiences and visits to the Churches.

It will give the reader an idea of the range and variety of the activities of the World Council if I append a list of the Departments presenting reports at the last meeting at Lucknow (1953):

Report of the Commission on Faith and Order
Report of the Commission of the Churches on International Affairs
Report of the Study Department
Report of the Department of Inter-Church Aid and Service to Refugees
Report of the Youth Department
Report of the Ecumenical Institute
Report of the Commission on the Life and Work of Women in the Church
Report of the Secretariat for Evangelism
Report of the Joint Secretariat for East Asia
Report of the Committee on the Ecumenical History
Report of the Ecumenical Review

All reports are open for discussion, and some of them naturally at times give rise to vigorous debate. They are published afterwards in the Minutes, and some of them also in the *Ecumenical Review*. To follow their progress every year is to be aware of the Council's increasing responsibilities and expanding tasks.

It is, however, in the discussion of what are called the Main Themes that we get the clearest evidence of the development in thought. There are usually two. As it happens the choice of Themes has reflected each time the two comprehensive concerns of the Council, (a) of maintaining the fellowship of the Churches, and (b) of witnessing to the Kingship of Christ.

Chichester 1949

When the Central Committee met at Chichester in July 1949, there was a general discussion on the first Main Theme, 'What should the Churches expect from the World Council of Churches?' This was exploratory in character, but both points mentioned above received attention. It so happened, however, that the principle of 'witnessing to the Kingship of Christ' had already been noted, almost by accident, at the short meeting at Woudschoeten in 1948. News arrived, just as the Assembly broke up, that a member of the Central Committee, Bishop Ordass, elected a delegate to the Assembly from the Hungarian Lutheran Church, had been arrested and imprisoned. Much time was given at Woudschoeten to a discussion of the situation. In the end it was decided to send a letter to the President of the Council of Hungary, Mr Dinnyes Lajos, expressing the grave concern of the World Council at the news, and asking certain questions. It was also decided to make a public protest in the event of an unsatisfactory or negative reply. The reply of the President was unsatisfactory, and the public protest was made in October 1948.

Totalitarian Doctrine

At Chichester the discussion on the second Main Theme 'Contemporary Issues of Religious Liberty', started with an account of the situation in Hungary and in other countries in Eastern Europe. There was a vigorous debate in which Professor Hromadka (Czechoslovakia), Dr Fry (U.S.A.),

Professor Alivisatos (Greece), Bishop Fjellbu (Norway), Dr Niemöller (Germany), and others took part. All agreed that a statement should be made; but that in such statement the totalitarian doctrine, and not the Communist economic system, should be condemned. It was also pointed out by various speakers that the Church everywhere should protest against exploitation by any kind of state or society. In the end a statement was issued which, after strong condemnation of the totalitarian doctrine, said:

We call statesmen and all men who in every nation seek social justice to consider this truth: a peaceful and stable order can only be built upon foundations of righteousness, of right relations between man and God and between man and man. Only the recognition that man has ends and loyalties beyond the State will ensure true justice to the human person. Religious freedom is the condition and guardian of all true freedom. We declare the duty and the right of the Church to preach the Word of God and to proclaim the will of God. We appeal to the Churches to interpret and apply God's will to all realms of life. We warn the Churches in all lands against the danger of being exploited for worldly ends. In the countries where the State is antagonistic to the Christian religion or indeed wherever full religious freedom is denied, we ask all Christians to remember that the liberty which they receive from their Lord cannot be taken away by the violence or threat of any worldly power, or destroyed by suffering. Therefore we urge the Churches to bear clear corporate witness to the truth in Christ and their ministers to continue to preach the whole Gospel. We urge all Christians to stand firm in their faith, to uphold Christian principles in practical life and to secure Christian teaching for their children.

The Committee at the same time asked that the subject of Religious Liberty in relation to dominant religious communities should be placed upon the agenda for their next meeting.

Toronto 1950

In 1950 the Central Committee met at Toronto (Canada). It took 'Dominant Religions and Religious Liberty' as one of its Main Themes. A valuable survey was presented by the officers of the Commission of the Churches on International Affairs. The Central Committee resolved[1]:

(1) To declare its opposition to all practices by which governments, Churches, or other agencies curb the exercise of religious freedom; to call upon the Churches to disseminate information and to take individual and collective action for promoting in their own countries conditions under which religious freedom may be fully practised; and, further, to make representation regarding infringements to the religious authorities which have jurisdiction in the countries concerned.

(2) To encourage the development of a comprehensive and coordinated programme of action, national and international, and thereby to pursue affirmative, preventive, and remedial measures for promoting the observance of religious freedom for all men.

The Church, the Churches and the World Council of Churches

The two other Main Themes at Toronto were the 'Ecclesiological Significance of the World Council of Churches', and 'the Nature and Theme of the Second Assembly'. The former of these arose out of a very definite need for answers to be given to certain fundamental questions about the implications of membership in the Council, and for the removal of some stubborn misunderstanding.

A document had been prepared by the General Secretary, with the help of criticisms from theologians of many confessions. After revision by a sub-committee, it was presented to the whole body, and gave rise to a most frank and realistic debate. The crux of the discussion was the attitude of the member Churches to one another. It was a matter of principle with some Churches – not only the Orthodox – that they should regard other Churches as essentially incomplete. Other Churches, notably those of the Free Church tradition, disputed the right of any Church to tell other Churches that they were not full and true Churches. There were still other

1. See also pp. 124–6 [ch. 12].

Churches which expressed surprise at the Free Church reaction. As Pierre Maury (Reformed Church of France) put it, 'I do not consider my own Church a full and true Church. Nor the "High Churches" either! Nor the Roman Church! Why then should any family of Churches object because that fact is so stated in this document?'

The document, under the title *The Church, the Churches and the World Council of Churches*, must be studied as a whole. It sets out what the World Council is *not*. It is not a 'super-Church'. It is not a negotiator of unions. It is not based on any particular conception of the Church, or doctrine of the nature of Church unity. It does not assume that by becoming a member a Church treats its own conception of the Church as merely relative.

As it was on the positive side that the chief difficulties arose in the debate, the 'Assumptions underlying the World Council of Churches' must be set out more fully. The first three assumptions are stated thus:

(1) The member Churches of the Council believe that conversation, co-operation and common witness of the Churches must be based on the common recognition that Christ is the Divine Head of the Body.

(2) The member Churches of the World Council believe on the basis of the New Testament that the Church of Christ is one.

(3) The member Churches recognize that the membership of the Church of Christ is more inclusive than the membership of their own Church-body. They seek, therefore, to enter into living contact with those outside their own ranks who confess the Lordship of Christ.

The crucial paragraphs are those which immediately follow:

(4) The member Churches of the World Council consider the relationship of other Churches to the Holy Catholic Church which the Creeds profess as a subject for mutual consideration. Nevertheless, membership does not imply that each Church must regard the other member Churches as Churches in the true and full sense of the word.

(5) The member Churches of the World Council recognize in other Churches elements of the true Church. They consider that this mutual recognition obliges them to enter into a serious conversation with each other in the hope that these elements of truth will lead to the recognition of the full truth and to unity based on the full truth.

This section of the document goes on to emphasize the facts that the member Churches are willing to consult together in seeking to learn of the Lord Jesus Christ of the witness He would have them bear to the world in His name; that there is a solidarity with each other implied in common membership, involving mutual assistance and the avoidance of unfriendly actions; and that all enter into a spiritual relationship which they seek to learn from each other for the building up of the Body of Christ.

None of these positive assumptions, it is pointed out, implied in the existence of the World Council, is in conflict with the teachings of member Churches. No Church therefore need fear that the idea of entering into the World Council involves any danger of denying its heritage.

The Second Assembly

Much time was given to a discussion on the nature and theme of the Second Assembly. It was recognized that a great deal would turn both on the choice of the right theme, and the preparations made for its discussion when the Assembly met. Various suggestions were offered in a general debate. The essential problem was to strike a proper balance between the internal family matters of the World Council, and the issues in the contemporary world. After further full discussion it was agreed that the Main Theme of the Assembly should be along the lines of the affirmation that *Jesus Christ as Lord is the only Hope both of the Church and the World*; and that the Subsidiary Themes should be considered in relation to this central Theme.

The Korean War

The Toronto meeting was also notable for a discussion on the outbreak of the war in Korea. War broke out on 25 June 1950. The Central Committee met on 9 July. The Amsterdam Assembly had declared, 'there will certainly be a clear obligation for the Council to speak out when vital issues concerning all the Churches and the whole world are at stake'; and again, 'the nations of the world must acknowledge the rule of Law'. The United Nations is the only legal international authority in the world. A neutral international Commission had been on the scene in Korea at the time war broke out. The members of the Central Committee were convinced that it was their duty in the circumstances to bear their witness that the Churches were concerned with order in the world; and, that though not partisan, they could not remain neutral when a basic principle of human relationships was at stake. The expression of such convictions, however, did not mean that the World Council made common cause with one bloc against another bloc, or was not determined to maintain the closest possible personal relationships between the Churches living under different regimes.

The Central Committee decided to issue a statement, which was adopted unanimously, with the exception of the second sentence in the third paragraph (referring to a police measure) which was carried by forty-five votes to two.

In the first paragraph of the statement the Central Committee expressed its deep concern, and called upon its members, as a world-wide Christian fellowship, to pray for Korea and bear witness to Christ as the Lord of all life and Prince of Peace. The second and the next three paragraphs are as follows:

An act of aggression has been committed. The United Nations Commission in Korea, the most objective witness available, asserts that 'all evidence points to a calculated, co-ordinated attack prepared and launched with secrecy' by the North Korean troops.

Armed attack as an instrument of national policy is wrong. We therefore commend the United Nations, an instrument of world order, for its prompt decision to meet this aggression and for authorizing a police measure which every member nation should support. At the same time, governments must press individually and through the United Nations for a just settlement by negotiation and conciliation.

The enforced division of a people in Korea or elsewhere is a bitter result of the divided world. It violates fundamental rights and increases the threat to peace. The United Nations has attempted to establish a free, united, and independent Korea within the community of nations. Every opportunity which may arise from the present tragic situation must be used to gain this end.

The Korean situation need not be the beginning of a general war. We must not regard world-wide conflict as inevitable. Any tendency to irresponsible fatalism should be resisted. We stand for a just peace under the rule of law and must seek peace by expanding justice and by attempting to reconcile contending world powers. . . .

The Committee's action was the subject afterwards of a good deal of criticism, much of which was due to misunderstanding and imperfect reports. The international situation remained critical. At the meeting of the Executive Committee on 31 January – 1 February 1951, it was again closely surveyed, and a letter, pastoral in character, was sent out to all member Churches. The letter reminded the member Churches of the double task of the World Council in both maintaining fellowship between Christian Churches, and giving concrete witness to the Kingship of Christ; of the grievous deterioration in the international situation; of the duty of all the Churches to champion peace with justice; and of the special duty belonging to those Churches which have real opportunities of influencing government policies.

Rolle 1951

The discussion continued at the meeting of the Central Committee at Rolle (Switzerland) in August 1951. There a letter from Dr T. C. Chao, dated 28 April 1951, was read, resigning his office as Joint President. 'As a patriotic Chinese I must protest against the Toronto message, which sounds so much like the voice of Wall Street . . . I can no longer be one of the Presidents of the World Council. . . . Therefore I resign from the office. . . . In so doing I want to say that I have complete freedom to affirm my faith in and my loyalty to Jesus Christ, my Lord and Saviour.' Dr Chao is one of the most distinguished Christians in China. He has always been a great supporter of the ecumenical movement, and has refused to take a stand against it. He was Dean of the School of Religion, Yenching University, Peiping. But he has now lost that post, and lives in retirement.

In Times of Tension

The Main Themes at Rolle were 'The Role of the World Council of Churches in Times of Tension', and 'The Calling of the Church to Mission and Unity'. The debate on the former was notable for the evidence it gave of the ability of spokesmen of conflicting views to speak with complete frankness and charity in a World Council atmosphere. The protagonists were Bishop Berggrav (Norway) and Bishop Bereczky (Hungary). No one who was present in the two closed sessions, and listened to the appeals of one Bishop, and to the response of the other, will ever forget them. The spirit of the discussion may be perceived from an illustration given by Bishop Berggrav, and published in the report of a large portion of his speech in the *Ecumenical Review* for October 1951.

In the summer of 1947 tension between Holland and Indonesia reached the peak just as the World Conference of Christian Youth assembled in Oslo. In the crowded assembly hall you could feel the tension like electricity in the air. A Dutchman stood up and spoke, proposing that the Dutch and Indonesian delegates should meet in private and listen to each other and pray together. They did. The next day the atmosphere in the hall completely changed. There was no tension, no electricity, any more. Why? Had they been able to agree on all points? To agree is never the decisive thing. The decisive thing is that you get the whole matter under God. What they had experienced was that Christ was the common Master above the dispute.

The discussion of the other Main Theme was based on a draft document on the Missionary and Ecumenical Calling of the Church. It was pointed out that the missionary and ecumenical callings belonged to each other, and were complementary. Modern missions were born in the knowledge of Christ as Lord over the whole world, and are the responsibility of the whole Church. The document stressed the close connexion of the missionary or evangelistic task of the Church with the call for unity, and urged the necessity of a translation of this connexion into more concrete terms so far as organization was concerned, particularly in a much closer relationship between the International Missionary Council and the World Council. The document was remitted for further comment and study to the International Missionary Council and to the Joint Committee of the World Council and the I.M.C. with a view to a further report.

Lucknow 1953

The last meeting of the Central Committee was held at Lucknow. As the date of the Second Assembly drew nearer, the conviction grew that it would be a grave mistake for the Assembly to meet a second time in the West (as proposed) unless the Central Committee had already held a regular meeting in Asia. It was resolved, for reasons of expense, to omit the meeting due for the summer of 1952, and to accept the invitation of Miss Sarah Chakko (who had succeeded Dr Chao as Joint President) to meet in the Isabella Thoburn College, Lucknow, from 31 December 1952, to 8 January

1953. It was also urged that at this meeting a special effort should be made to bring the Asian situation in a very definite way before the members of the Central Committee.

There can be no two opinions as to the impact made by the Asian situation on the whole membership through the Lucknow meeting. Prime Minister Nehru gave an address to the members, in which he analysed the world situation. Dr Radhakrishnan, Vice-President of the Republic of India, paid a visit, and answered informally the many questions put to him. And there was both a remarkably full attendance from the older Churches, and an outstanding representation of the Churches of Asia, including India, Pakistan, Ceylon, Burma, Indonesia, Japan, Iran, and the Philippines.

The three Main Themes were 'The Two Primary Goals of the Ecumenical Movement – Mission and Unity'; 'The Relevance of the Christian Hope to Our Time'; and 'The Asian Situation as a Concern of Christians everywhere'.

The Asian Situation

As the General Secretary put it afterwards, their experience at Lucknow led members to reconsider many of their more or less fixed opinions. It came home to those who had travelled from the Western countries that, unlike most of the West, Asia was in a state of seeking and finding new solutions for old problems. The spokesmen of the Asian Churches challenged the static conceptions which are too often characteristic of the older Churches. The need for unity was continually emphasized by representatives of the Churches of Asia, as well as the need of social justice and racial equality. And so in a Letter to the Member Churches, issued by the Central Committee, an appeal was made to older and younger Churches alike:

Churches all over the world must ask how they can help the people of Asia in their efforts to attain a standard of living which meets basic human needs, and in their search for a more just social and economic order. The Church in Asia has the crucial task of helping to provide the true moral and spiritual dynamic for the people longing for social justice and peace. Without this dynamic their longing cannot be realized and may easily be betrayed by false hopes. To meet these needs, the full support of the Christian community in under-developed countries must be rallied behind the efforts of their Governments and people to tackle their own economic problems. The Churches in the more developed countries must urge their peoples and Governments to do everything possible to strengthen programmes of technical assistance, without which such efforts in Asia cannot succeed.

Again, with regard to unity, note should be taken of the emphasis laid in this same Letter on the duty of the older Churches in the matter of understanding freedom and continuing support:

No one can enter today into the Asian scene without realizing at every hand the urgency with which many of the Churches and Christian people are crying for unity. Where Christians find themselves as a small minority in the midst of vast communities of non-Christian people the call of God to all of us to seek for unity is powerfully reinforced by the demands and circumstances of the situation, and by their own task of witness.

There are dangers in this very sense of urgency which cannot be disregarded. Unity may sometimes be looked upon as a solution of all problems. It may be sought without due regard for truth in doctrine and soundness in order. But, having said this, we feel bound to state that the Churches of the West are called to show great understanding and a readiness to give full freedom and continuing support to their brethren in the East as they seek to find God's purpose for them in their own time and place.

As this was the last meeting of the Central Committee before the Second Assembly to be held at Evanston, U.S.A., a good deal of time was given to the preparations. The Theme for that Assembly, 'Christ the Hope of the World', had been chosen at Toronto in 1950, and much work had been done upon it since that date by a special Commission of Theologians of many confessions, meeting in successive years for a week at a time. The first Report which had been presented in 1951 disclosed considerable differences of opinion, particularly with regard to the Second Coming of Christ. The second Report was a substantial piece of work, dealing with the nature and relevance of the Christian Hope, and its connexion with the Utopias of today; and noted that one reason for the rise of extreme apocalyptic and millenarian beliefs is the virtual disappearance among many Christians and in the preaching of many Churches of the distinctive Christian Hope in Christ's coming again. But this subject will be more fully treated in the last chapter of this book.

Letter to the President of the United Nations Assembly

The Korean war also once more confronted the Committee, which was meeting nine days after the adjournment of the United Nations, which had broken up with a sense of frustration, no armistice yet having been reached. A group of members was appointed early in the proceedings to consider whether there was any action which the Central Committee could properly take. In the end the Committee decided to address a letter through its chairman direct to the President of the United Nations Assembly, Mr Lester Pearson (Canada) expressing the concern of the World Council. This was a new departure for the Central Committee; but all agreed to the proposal in the special emergency. The letter was cabled, and received wide publicity. Its central section was as follows:

The Central Committee wishes me to say how greatly it appreciates the efforts of the United Nations to overcome what is apparently the one remaining obstacle to the conclusion of an armistice in Korea. It regrets that no plan has so far been found acceptable to all parties. It most earnestly urges the United Nations to persevere in its efforts to resolve the conflict by a truce which will safeguard prisoners of war against forcible repatriation or forcible detention.

The question of repatriation may not be the only obstacle to the conclusion of agreements to end fighting, and other steps may have to be taken. The Central Committee therefore welcomes the expressed willingness of the highest authorities of certain great powers to hold personal discussion and trusts that the essential preliminary conditions of successful consultation may be satisfied.

The immediate object for which the United Nations intervened has been fulfilled. There now remains the settlement of the Korean question with a view to the unification and independence of Korea. The Central Committee is far from underestimating the difficulties. But it is convinced that the only way to end the bloodshed in Korea and so hasten the solution not only of the Korean but also of wider questions is through negotiated settlements. A deep sense of responsibility therefore prompts this appeal to the United Nations to guard against any extension of the conflict and to persist unceasingly in the promotion of negotiations until success is achieved. It commends the more widespread use in international conferences of an umpire.

The Central Committee of the World Council of Churches is also aware that the serious economic needs of many countries in different parts of the world especially in Asia cry out for attention. It appreciates the notable work done through technical assistance and in other humanitarian ways by the United Nations and urges the nations unitedly to devote their resources to meet this call. But in this grave and perilous hour the breaking of the deadlock in Korea is the immediate and essential step to these wider constructive activities.

It was unanimously adopted, and published, together with a call to Church people to pray for the establishment of a just and lasting peace. The action of the Central Committee was all the more significant when it is remembered that it was taken at a meeting with a large attendance of delegates from Asian Churches, and also when Bishop Peter was present as a delegate from the Reformed Church of Hungary.

This brief summary of some of the main features of the work of the Central Committee between the two Assemblies must not end without laying very special emphasis on the visits paid to Churches all over the world by the officers of the World Council; and on the work of the staff. To see the World Council of Churches in a visible form, in the persons of its leaders, is essential to the strengthening of the hold of the World Council on its member Churches, and to the maintaining of the general Christian fellowship. Such visits have been paid throughout these six years, with great profit, by the Joint Presidents, the Chairman and Vice-Chairman, by members of the Executive Committee and by members of the staff. Australia, New Zealand, South America, Palestine, India, Pakistan, Ceylon, Indonesia, North Africa, South Africa, as well as Hungary and Czechoslovakia, have all received visits, and given the visitors a wonderful welcome. I must pay a special tribute to the leadership of the General Secretary, Dr W. A. Visser 't Hooft. At the age of 24 he was the youngest participant in the Stockholm Conference of 1925. He was General Secretary of the World Student Christian Federation from 1932 to 1938. He was appointed General Secretary to the Provisional Committee of the World Council in 1938. For nearly thirty years he has been intimately connected with the persons and activities of the ecumenical movement in all parts of the world. He has been untiring in his travels, outstanding in the friendship he has brought and in the inspiration he has everywhere given, and brilliant in his theological insight, and in the guidance he has provided in the planning of the whole work and policy of the World Council of Churches from Amsterdam to the present day.

10

FAITH AND ORDER

THE first function assigned to the World Council of Churches in its constitution is 'to carry on the work of the two world movements for Faith and Order and for Life and Work'. As already explained in an earlier chapter, the Faith and Order movement had its source in the desire of certain pioneer churchmen before the First World War to bring about a conference for the consideration of questions of faith and order in a reunited Church. It was therefore specially concerned with doctrines and the ministry. The Life and Work movement arose directly out of the First World War, and sprang from a combination of a passion for Christian unity with a passion for Peace and for Social Justice. Its leaders were deeply impressed by the urgent need of common action by all the Churches, without tarrying for the solution of the age-long controversies which divided them. 'Is it necessary,' Archbishop Söderblom asked, 'to go into the question of our different creeds, views, and customs, when the great thing in common really exists in our hearts, namely, obedience to the voice of our Lord? Our own work in his service as well as the distress of our generation renders systematic co-operation imperative.'

Many of the same Church leaders were in both movements, but they were also conscious of their distinctive tasks. Accordingly, when Mr Robert Gardiner, the Secretary of the Faith and Order movement, wrote to the leaders of the Life and Work movement suggesting that the two World Conferences should be held at the same place and at about the same time, Archbishop Söderblom and Dr Henry Atkinson on behalf of the Executive Committee of Life and Work in session at Hälsingborg, 12–15 August 1922, replied:

We are concerned with service, and we believe that by serving the co-operation of the churches we shall break down prejudices and create a spirit of fellowship which will render the accomplishment of the aims of the Faith and Order movement less difficult to achieve.

Meanwhile, we are of the opinion that the two movements had better be kept distinct: Life and Work confining itself in the main to the co-operation of the Churches in the application of the Spirit and Teaching of Christ to social, national and international relationships, while Faith and Order devotes its attention to the ultimate but more remote goal of unity in Doctrine and Church Order.

So Life and Work went forward by itself; and the first World Conference of the Churches since the Great Schism was the Stockholm Conference on Life and Work in 1925. Faith and Order followed in 1927 at Lausanne. But in spite of this taking of separate paths, it soon appeared that complete separation could not be maintained. Life and Work discovered that theology after all had something to say to social and international affairs; and that matters of faith and order could not be completely excluded from its field. Faith and Order also found rather later that social and cultural factors played quite a large part in Church divisions. It was, I think, the increasing awareness of this truth, as well as the realization that the support of the Churches would be more easily won for a single movement working through distinctive departments than for two movements working in entire separation from one another, which led to the decision in 1937 by both bodies to approve the formation of a World Council of Churches. The requirement from the Faith and Order side that its distinctive position must be clearly safeguarded in the new Council, caused special provision to be made in the Constitution for a Faith and Order Commission in accord with its principles.

A Continuing Conversation

There have been three World Conferences on Faith and Order in the last thirty years: Lausanne (1927), Edinburgh (1937), and Lund (1952). Each has been a particular stage in a continuing conversation. Some of the guiding principles of Faith and Order are that in its conferences no steps shall be taken towards reunion, no schemes be formulated, no decision concerning disputed questions of faith and order be endorsed as the opinion of the Conference. The reason for this principle is that the whole aim of the movement has been to draw all Churches into an ecumenical conversation. No Church must be made to feel that it must stay away or withdraw from a conference because otherwise it would have to endorse something disloyal to its own conviction, or be exhibited as a minority which was an obstacle to progress.

The Conferences have been singularly useful in bringing divines and Church leaders together from the most diverse Churches, and often from countries with the most diverse cultures. When the participants have met they have been able to listen as well as talk, to discover or rediscover each other's Churches, and to compare the results of the latest theological research in a way quite beyond the reach of a long-range correspondence between scholars personally unknown to one another. Nearly all who have attended have also shared a profound spiritual experience. They have enjoyed a sense of extraordinary fellowship, and so the beginning of a new consciousness, however dim, that they belong to a Christian world community. With this there has often come a steadily deepening sense of the wrongness of divisions, and of the need of doing all that can be done by study and prayer to help forward the unity of the Church.

Each Conference has had its own characteristics and leaders. Great men are the guideposts and landmarks in the ecumenical movement. So, besides recording a particular stage on the road to unity, each Conference has been notable for a special personal leadership.

The Lausanne Conference

There can be no question of the dominating impression made on the delegates to the first World Conference at Lausanne by Charles Henry Brent, Bishop of Western New York since 1918. He was a son of Canada, but started his ministry in Buffalo, U.S.A. He was consecrated Bishop of the Philippines at the age of 38. I knew him well as a frequent guest at Lambeth and Canterbury, where he and Archbishop and Mrs Randall Davidson were devoted to one another. He had a fine presence, a serene and smiling look. He was a man of deep prayer; a lover of children, and with an extraordinary influence on all sorts of people in politics, business, and the Services. He was an eloquent champion of the unity of the Church, and of Justice and Peace among the nations. As he was also the prime mover for a Faith and Order Conference in 1910,[1] it was peculiarly right that he should be elected the first President. Imagine the effect on the congregation in Lausanne Cathedral when, in a voice remarkable both for beauty and power, he began his sermon with these words: 'We are here at the urgent behest of Jesus Christ. We have come with willing feet. All the prayers and desires and labour of seventeen years meet in this hour.' It was Bishop Brent certainly, with Dr A. E. Garvie as deputy Chairman, who carried the Conference, and imparted an enthusiasm to those taking part.

The great achievement of Lausanne was to sound the call to unity, and to make Christians see its significance. Delegates were genuinely surprised to discover the amount of common ground; many as a result underestimated the stubbornness of the differences disclosed. Looking back in

1. See pp. 20–1 [ch. 2].

1953, Archbishop Brilioth (Sweden), the present President, writes: 'The reunited Church was spoken of as a tangible reality, as something that might perhaps not be realized in the present generation, but still was an event to be reckoned with as possible in a not too distant future. A certain tendency to gloss over differences by formulas that could be interpreted differently was perhaps not absent during this stage.'

Even so, the delegates of the Lutheran Churches made a statement concerning their difficulties with regard to the authority and formulation of certain Reports. The difficulty of the task of Faith and Order was also underlined by a long declaration made by Orthodox delegates which, while full of goodwill for the purpose of the Conference, regretted 'that the bases assumed for the foundation of the Reports which are to be submitted to the vote of the Conference are not consistent with the principles of the Orthodox Church which we represent.'

The Edinburgh Conference

The second World Conference took place at Edinburgh in 1937. Many of the delegates who had arrived as strangers at Lausanne met at Edinburgh as friends. Here the outstanding personality was Bishop Brent's successor, Archbishop William Temple, Archbishop of York. He had been at Lausanne, and had from the first taken a leading part at the meetings of the Continuation Committee, of which he became Chairman when Bishop Brent died in 1929. He came all fresh from presiding over the Committee of thirty-five, which made recommendations for the formation of a World Council of Churches. At Edinburgh all his remarkable gifts of conciliation, spiritual leadership, of speaking and drafting, of serenity and humour, had full scope. When he died so unexpectedly in 1944, he was by far the leading figure in the ecumenical movement. The loss created by his death is incalculable: but at Edinburgh he was seen as the prophet of the Universal Church. Very unlike him in temperament, but prominent in debate, and, while broad in outlook, highly dogmatic in speech, was another Anglican, Dr A. C. Headlam, Bishop of Gloucester.

The Orthodox delegation was smaller than it had been at Lausanne. It made another declaration, in which its reservations were again expressed. There was no representation of the German Evangelical Church, by order of the Nazi Government; and while Lutheran theologians from Sweden, like Bishop Aulen and Professor Nygren, made fine contributions, the revival in biblical theology did not hit the Edinburgh Conference with anything like the force it should have had. Differences became clearer: but the note of unity still seemed to prevail. A special tribute has been paid by Archbishop Brilioth to the work done by the Commission on the Doctrine of Grace, under the chairmanship of Bishop Headlam. And there was another valuable Report on the Ministry and the Sacraments.

The Lund Conference

The third World Conference was held at Lund, Sweden, in 1952. The President there was Archbishop Brilioth. In him too a special kind of personal influence found expression. He is an admirable scholar, well known for his works on Church History, both Swedish and Anglican, and a fine book on Eucharistic Worship. He is an able Church statesman, and not only successor to Archbishop Söderblom in the Primacy of the Church of Sweden, but his kinsman as son-in-law, and his disciple in his ecumenical ideals.

The Lund Conference was remarkable for two challenging reminders. One came from Professor Joseph Hromadka of Czechoslovakia, speaking of the tremendous challenge which is presented by the revolutionary and socialistic ideology and its salutary effect. 'We are realizing what it means (*theologically* speaking) to walk between life and death. Every word and category, every traditional Church activity has to be rethought, reinterpreted, re-evaluated as to its integrity and relevance.'

The other was a statement by representatives of the younger Churches, from lands in which Church union negotiations have either been completed or are in progress, asking their fellow-delegates to remember 'that unprecedented situations cannot be dealt with in every detail by the precedents of Church history'; and also appealing to them 'to encourage similar schemes of union amongst yourselves and your kindred overseas'.

The Lund Conference made important recommendations on ways of worship, the nature of the Church, and intercommunion. It gave a particular emphasis to the importance of the non-theological (i.e. social and cultural) factors in our divisions. It also revealed a growth in the tenacity with which different Churches maintained their distinctive positions. More important than anything else, it demonstrated that a new stage in the ecumenical discussion had been reached. So far the main method had been to compare the convictions of the Churches. Lund asked the Churches to look afresh at the whole fundamental question of the relation of the Church to Christ and showed that by going to Christ as the centre of our faith we have the greatest opportunity of meeting each other.

The Faith and Order Commission

Subject to the approval of the Assembly at Evanston in August 1954, the following functions were assigned at Lund to the Faith and Order Commission in the World Council of Churches:

(i) To proclaim the essential oneness of the Church of Christ and to keep prominently before the World Council and the Churches the obligation to manifest that unity and its urgency for the work of evangelism.

(ii) To study questions of faith, order, and worship with the relevant social, cultural, political, racial and other factors in their bearing on the unity of the Church.

(iii) To study the theological implications of the existence of the ecumenical movement.

(iv) To study matters in the present relationship of the Churches to one another which cause difficulties and need theological clarification.

(v) To provide information concerning actual steps taken by the Churches towards reunion.

It was again made plain that the main work of the Commission is to draw Churches out of isolation into conference, in which none is to be asked to be disloyal to or compromise its convictions; that it has no right to formulate schemes and tell Churches what they ought to do; but that its work is simply to act as the handmaid of the Churches in the preparatory work of clearing away misunderstandings, discussing obstacles, and issuing reports for the consideration of the Churches. The Commission consists of 85 members, appointed by the Assembly, with up to 15 additional members nominated by itself for appointment by the Central Committee, making a total of 100.

The importance of Faith and Order in the whole context of the World Council is beyond dispute. There are four particular ways in which this stands out. (1) It emphasizes the significance of theology in the whole life of the Church; side by side with the Study Department of the World Council at Geneva, itself deeply concerned with a true theology and biblical foundations. (2) It will keep the Churches well informed with regard to union movements. One of the most heartening facts in the whole contemporary life of the Churches is the achievement of Church unions, notably that of the Church of South India; and the steady increase in Church union negotiations. (3) It will call all Christians, especially in the Week of Prayer for Church Unity (18–25 January), to join with their fellows of many confessions and tongues in fervent prayer to God that He will remove the barriers which separate His people from one another. (4) It will remind the Churches that co-operation is not enough; that the fellowship of Churches in the World Council of Churches is a beginning, not an end; and point to a true unity which will make it clear to the whole world that as there can be only one Body of Christ, so there is only one Body which is the Church of His people.

II

INTER-CHURCH AID AND SERVICE TO REFUGEES

THERE is no way in which the fellowship of the Churches can be more clearly expressed than when the stronger help the weaker in times of need. In the very beginning of the Christian Church, the Churches in Greece were taught by S. Paul to come to the aid of their impoverished fellow-churchmen in Jerusalem. Throughout Christian history this duty has been recognized as an integral part of the missionary work of the Church. Therefore when the World Council of Churches came to be formed, it was only natural that the same principle should be followed by its member Churches in their relations with one another.

The principle may be simply described as that of Inter-Church Aid. It was first applied as between Protestant Churches helping Protestant Churches in another country, by the organization founded by Dr Adolf Keller in 1922, and known as the Central European Bureau of Inter-Church Aid. This had its headquarters in Geneva, and offices in New York; and it did invaluable pioneer work between the two World Wars. When the Second World War came, the officers of the Provisional Committee of the World Council, as we have already observed, felt that a large-scale plan involving the member Churches generally should be set on foot.

I have already described the initiation of that work, resulting from a visit to Geneva by Dr S. McCrea Cavert on behalf of the American Churches. What was proposed was a Department of the World Council of Churches to help in 'reconstruction of Christian institutions in Europe'. The task of reconstruction was conceived as an ecumenical task in which all the member Churches would participate to the utmost of their ability, with the common objective of re-building the life of the whole fellowship of member Churches. This would mean that the Churches would agree to co-ordinate their activities in order to make certain that all needy Churches received adequate help and that the autonomy and desires of receiving Churches were fully considered.

Much preliminary work had to be done before the war ended. This was a field in which those in Britain or in other countries who had had contact with the Churches in Germany took a deep interest. I was myself an active partner, working with others in different Churches, in the setting up in Britain of the inter-Church body known as 'Christian Reconstruction in Europe', which appealed for £1,000,000, and before it closed (in 1950) had raised and spent a total of £1,237,450. C.R.E. was one of a large number of similar committees in many countries, notably U.S.A., Sweden, and Switzerland, with which the Department at Geneva established contact. Information was also obtained from Churches in those countries which had suffered most through the war. The first meeting of the Committee of the Department was held at Geneva on 15 May 1945, with Dr Koechlin, President of the Swiss Church Federation, as Chairman, and Dr. J. Hutchinson Cockburn (Scotland) as senior secretary.

Two Responsibilities

From the very first the Department has had two functions, (1) the co-ordinating of work done by the Churches in the total field, thus avoiding overlapping, and securing and passing on information about needs which might otherwise be overlooked, as direct aid was constantly being given by

Church to Church from funds raised by the Churches; and (2) the undertaking of special projects in its own name, through funds directly contributed to Geneva for this purpose. The greater amount of the money raised by the Churches was spent on their own projects, guided and co-ordinated by the Department. But the very effectiveness of the projects set on foot by the different Churches depended and depends on the continuing work of the Department with its own projects in the field of Inter-Church Aid, and its own service to refugees.

In the space at my disposal I can only give a bare outline of the various activities for which the World Council has been responsible from 1945 to the present day. But it is instructive to observe the development from (1) the first phase, which dealt with an immediate post-war emergency, and was limited to the reconstruction of Church life in the stricken countries of Europe, to (2) the second phase, where Inter-Church Aid was seen as a permanent obligation to assist Churches, still only in Europe, in days when the witness and indeed the very existence of the Church was being challenged; and (3) the third phase, when the Department's duties are seen to extend outside the bounds of Europe, and are linked with the missionary work of the Church through the International Missionary Council.

(1) *Immediate Post-War Reconstruction*

During the first phase, May 1945 to August 1948, very large sums of money were spent on relief and rehabilitation. The member Churches, especially in America, had their own wide-ranging operations, co-ordinated by the Department. But taking the World Council of Churches' own specific undertakings as financed by member Churches in U.S.A., Britain, Switzerland, Canada, New Zealand, and Sweden, the heaviest expenditure in the years 1945–8 was 1,088,300 dollars on the provision of temporary churches, some made of wood, and others of wood with walls built of rubble. The next heaviest was 900,000 dollars for salaries of pastors and clergy of different denominations. The total, including the rebuilding of Christian orphanages, hospitals, schools, homes for the aged, for these three years was 3,905,500 dollars. All the countries occupied during the war were recipients, without discrimination. But perhaps the most remarkable example of the 'love of the brethren' developed by the Churches through the World Council was the widespread and generous help given to Germany by the Churches, in U.S.A. most of all, but also by those in Britain and other countries. Those who visited Germany, as I did, in the very early post-war years could not fail to observe both the liberality of the giving, and the quality of the personal approach.

(2) *The Permanent Obligation*

The work of the Department entered upon a new phase after Amsterdam, with Dr Robert Mackie as Director, in succession to Dr Cockburn. The emergency task of post-war reconstruction gave way to the permanent obligation of Inter-Church Aid. This by no means meant that all the reconstruction that was possible had been done. Far from it. But it was the ongoing task of all the member Churches which was now at the centre of the picture. The great spiritual struggle concerning the nature of man was raging, and the vital need was for all Churches to help one another to greater ardour in the fulfilment of their spiritual role. A World Council of Churches which refused to have a Department of Inter-Church Aid on a permanent basis was unthinkable. And there was an increasingly urgent call from the refugees.

Certain important results followed. The word 'Recon-struction' disappeared from the title. The Department received the new and fuller name of 'Inter-Church Aid, and Service to Refugees'. The *aim* of the Department, in its present form, is 'to further, on an ecumenical basis, the renewal of the Churches through practical help which Churches may render one another, through the relief of human need, and through Service to Refugees'. The principal *function* of the Department is 'to provide, on the basis of mutual study and consultation, a total strategy of Inter-Church Aid and Service to Refugees in which the initiative and programmes of all Churches and national committees can be related to one another, and thus be given maximum usefulness'.

In 1952, when the second phase came to an end, the funds spent by member Churches on the whole of the transactions of Inter-Church Aid in Europe, including the value of contributed goods, such as clothing, basic foods, equipment for vocational training, etc., amounted to 8,500,000 dollars, of which 7,333,628 was contributed by the American Churches.

(3) *Extension beyond Europe*

The third phase followed soon after. The Department's activities are no longer to be limited to Europe, but must be conceived on a world scale, the International Missionary Council combining with the World Council to secure this. The movement of world events has made unified ecumenical action in meeting human needs and the challenge of formidable non-Christian forces more necessary than ever. As a result of much deliberation, the World Council of Churches and the International Missionary Council in 1953 both approved a plan for co-operation in Inter-Church Aid and Relief in countries outside Europe. It is important to observe that 'relief' is a term which covers the terrible needs of large masses of mankind in the countries of the younger Churches. Ordinary missionary channels are indeed inadequate for such a task: hence the significance of the new step taken on behalf of the World Council and the International Missionary Council together. We must also note the possibilities thus opened out, for co-operation in United Nations programmes of technical assistance for the economic and social development of under-developed territories.

Inter-Church Aid covers so large and varied a field that it is difficult to select one or two examples without seeming to be unfair to other branches. There is the work amongst youth – a fine illustration of which is the Youth Centre Agape, in northern Italy – the result of co-operation by many Churches and countries both in giving funds, and through the physical labour of their young people. There is a health and medical service, the bringing of clergy and Church workers as patients to recuperate in Switzerland, for example; the rest home for pastors at Casa Locarno; and the little known but valuable provision of medicine and special food parcels which are sent to different parts of Europe, especially Eastern Europe. What a joy it was to me, when, on receiving an appeal from an Orthodox Bishop in Eastern Europe – a friend of long standing, now old and ill and unable to leave his home – begging me to obtain some rare and expensive medicine for his niece as the one means of saving her life, I was able to secure its transmission to him at once, through Geneva.

A special contribution which has meant much in the permanent rebuilding of Church life is the service done by Inter-Church Aid to the Orthodox Churches in exile. The European Central Bureau for Relief, under Dr Adolf Keller, had given valuable assistance in pre-war days to the Russian Orthodox Academy in Paris, to Christians in Russia itself, and to Armenian institutions in Lebanon, and the Assyrian Church in Iraq. But this work of the World Council among the Orthodox in exile in so many places is something which has gone far further afield. When a well-known layman of the Russian emigration suddenly exclaimed at the meeting of the Central Committee at Toronto – 'Inter-Church Aid has its most genuinely ecumenical character when Protestants helped Orthodox!' – he went to the heart of the matter. It is really the case that the Orthodox Churches in exile owe their basic existence to the help given them by non-Orthodox Churches, largely through the Service to Refugees; and the feeling for the World Council on the part of these congregations of Orthodox in a wide variety of places is correspondingly great.

Then there is the fascinating story of Hong Kong. There are some 15,000 Russian Orthodox left in China, in a seemingly desperate situation. Their one possibility of freedom and a future is through Hong Kong, where, in the name of the World Council, Pastor Stumpf, a German Lutheran pastor, holds the life-line. From Hong Kong, 1,700 refugees have gone to South American countries where they have not only revivified the existing Orthodox parishes, but have started new ones. Andy Mouravieff, himself of Russian origin and Orthodox, works to find places for them there in close collaboration with Pastor Stumpf. And it is not only the Orthodox Churches in exile to which help goes. There is hardly a country in Eastern Europe in which the Orthodox Churches, and the Protestant Churches as well, do not rejoice at the visits of members of the staff of Inter-Church Aid, as they come with help and greeting, material succour of various kinds, and Christian fellowship.

Service to Refugees

Beyond all doubt the most urgent part of the Department's work at the present time is the Service to Refugees. Those who come under this general title include both pre-war and non-repatriable refugees, amounting to more than 1,500,000 persons. To these a vast new population of expellees and political fugitives has to be added as a result of the Potsdam

Agreement and other causes. Altogether the total number of refugees of all categories in Europe is estimated at 12,000,000 of whom 10,000,000 are in Western Germany. There are also 850,000 Arab refugees in Palestine, 350,000 expelled from Bulgaria in Turkey, and an incalculably large number in China, Korea, India, and Pakistan.

If I may be allowed a personal note, the work for refugees has long been a dominant concern of my own, from the days before the war, when, added to the refugee migrations from Turkey, Greece, and Bulgaria, to the Armenian and Assyrian deportations, to the Russian emigration and the flight from the rise of Fascist Governments in Italy and Spain, there came the host of Jewish and non-Aryan Christian refugees from Germany. Large numbers were able to reach Britain, the United States, France, and other countries. In Britain a Christian Council, including the Roman Catholics, was set up to help all refugees, whether Jewish or Christian, who were victims of the Nuremberg Laws. The Rev. M. E. Aubrey (Baptist), the Rev. Henry Carter (Methodist), Bishop David Mathew (R.C.), and I served together on the Council for a long while.

In 1946 the World Council set up an Ecumenical Refugee Commission, with the Rev. Henry Carter as its indefatigable and generous hearted chairman. Its special care was for refugees of the Protestant and Eastern Orthodox faiths, and for those with no faith at all. Later it came to be known as the 'Service to Refugees', under the direction, first of the Rev. Elfan Rees (now Geneva Secretary of the Commission of the Churches on International Affairs and general Adviser on Refugees), and then of Dr. Edgar Chandler.

The Personal Touch

There are millions of refugees, but they are all of them persons. The World Council of Churches is not only undertaking administrative tasks for the suffering masses, but dealing with the personal problems of individuals. I remember well a German Roman Catholic coming to see me before the war, when I was staying at Lambeth Palace for a meeting of Bishops, to tell me of the plight of his fellow-countrymen in Germany – some suffering for their politics, some for their religion, some for their race. He spoke of the thousands who longed to get out of Germany, and were trying to find a means of escape and a shelter. 'How,' I said, 'can a single person begin to try and help so many thousands?' But when I added, after a moment, 'Suppose one could help ten individuals; or suppose some committee (which was later formed) could manage to help a few hundreds, it would reduce the sum of human misery by just that amount!' 'Yes,' he said, 'that beginning of help would make the whole difference!'

It is in dealing with individuals, helping them in their personal problems, showing that they are not lost amongst the millions, that the workers for the World Council do so much, in addition to their general work of organization and relief. Here is a single illustration. A middle-aged Rumanian woman, who had been expelled from her country, and become a 'displaced person' in Germany, then was resettled in Persia by the World Council after six months of negotiation, with 127 letters to be written, most of them followed up by personal interviews. It is typical of thousands. The number of individual refugees whom the World Council has helped to find new homes in the United States, Australia, and elsewhere is at least 100,000! It has now in hand (January 1954) a further 25,000, whose dossiers it has prepared, in the hope of helping them to emigrate in a similar way. And while they are waiting, the World Council helps them by securing spiritual ministrations, and shelter, and material relief.

Political Action

Side by side with services such as those just described, the World Council has been greatly concerned with stimulating high-level political action on behalf of refugees, both in Europe and Asia. Three important conferences have been held: at Hamburg in 1949 (for refugees in Germany); at Salzburg in 1950 (for refugees in Austria); and at Beirut in 1951 (for refugees in Palestine).

In February 1949 the World Council called a Conference at Hamburg, attended by representatives of Occupying Powers and of German Governments and Churches. It was the first conference at which the actual situation of the refugees, its social, economic, and spiritual implications, was focused and studied in its full proportions. Many of the steps taken later at governmental and inter-governmental level had their origin in this meeting. It therefore stands out as perhaps the most significant of the Department's actions in this field, measured by the range of its results.

Palestine

In May 1951 the World Council and the International Missionary Council convened a conference at Beirut, to study the problem of the Palestine refugees. It was attended by Church delegates from the United States and Britain, together with leaders of the work of Churches and Missions in the Near East. All the delegates from outside spent two or three days before the conference began in visiting the refugee camps in the different areas, thus making first-hand contact with the problem set by the 850,000 Arab refugees from Israel. The Conference was convinced 'that there could be no permanent solution of the problem of the Palestinian refugees until there is a settlement of the outstanding political differences between the Arab States and Israel'. It added that 'such a settlement will have to contain provision for the return of a certain number of refugees to their original home', as well as 'a general plan of compensation for refugees whether they return or not'. In the meantime the Conference appealed to the Christian Churches to redouble their efforts for relief and rehabilitation. A Committee of the Near East Christian Council for Refugee Relief was set up, with local committees, and a full-time Executive Secretary was appointed. It is estimated that the total contribution of the Churches, in cash and in kind, to the service of the refugees, now exceeds 2,000,000 dollars per annum.

The Korean Emergency

When fighting ceased in Korea on the conclusion of a truce, it was not only the problem of prisoners of war, or a political settlement, that had to be solved. There were the millions of suffering people calling upon the charity of their fellow human beings to enable them to survive. A Relief Committee was already in existence, known as Korean Church World Service. After some negotiation, this became the Relief Committee of the Korean National Christian Council (one of the constituent Councils of the International Missionary Council), and was brought into official relationship with Inter-Church Aid and Service to Refugees. Members of an ecumenical staff are now at work in the country, including men and women from the United States, Canada, and Britain, as well as Koreans. New projects are being developed on behalf of widows, orphans and other groups which have suffered terribly. In August 1953 the Executive Committee of the World Council, meeting at Bossey, passed the following resolution:

The Executive Committee at its first meeting after the cessation of fighting in Korea upon the conclusion of a truce, noting that a way had been opened for an approach to the critical problems of political unification and effective rehabilitation by processes of negotiation and reconstruction; urged upon the member Churches their obligation to press their Governments to participate fully in all inter-government relief measures, and themselves to support through Christian liberality the Relief Committee of the National Christian Council of Korea in making its vital Christian contribution to the work of national reconstruction; and declared its intention to secure, through the Department of Inter-Church Aid and Service to Refugees, the widest possible co-operation of member Churches in working through Churches in both South and North Korea, always with the definite understanding that the distribution be in the hands of Church agencies, and that the identity of the giving Churches be freely disclosed.

It is a great encouragement that the British Churches are now responding to Korean needs, and that funds are coming in from various countries on the Continent. One of the workers in the 'Korean Operation' has sent a report from Pusan of work now going on, dated December 1953. He speaks of the large supplies of food and clothing from Church World Service, and the distribution being made to about 130 different destinations in South Korea, with the help of Korean pastors, sometimes living in a state of material poverty painful to see. He describes the primitive housing – 'a few feet of trodden earth for floor, a wall of scraps of wood with newspaper to staunch the gaps, and a roof of flattened-out cardboard boxes' ; and he ends his report with 'a story against ourselves':

Some gift parcels from Norway were in the warehouse and I was discussing with one of the staff how we should distribute them for Christmas, when he said he thought there was the donor's picture in each parcel. Thinking, office-fashion, of the work of individual acknowledgement that this would involve, I broke out, 'But that's impossible – all these parcels can't have their donor's picture in with them'. But in that I was wrong. For in each parcel there was a small picture, a portrait. *Of our Lord.*

Conclusion

The above gives a picture of the work on which the World Council Department of Inter-Church Aid and Service to Refugees is engaged. It shows Christian charity in action. Like the best administration it is all human and personal. It may be well to make a final point that the work of Service to Refugees, which is done complementary to and in association with United Nations agencies, is so well regarded by now that new Agencies for new tasks look to it automatically for the same help. Thus, when the International Refugee Organization (IRO), successor to the United Nations Relief and Rehabilitation Administration (UNRRA), closed down in 1951, the World Council became its residuary legatee for the care of refugees in Turkey, Ethiopia, Egypt, Iran, Japan, China, and the Philippines; and received grants amounting to 1,000,000 dollars to use on behalf of European refugees in these countries. The United Nations High Commissioner immediately got into touch with the World Council on taking up his appointment. The World Council is one of six major voluntary organizations to which the United Nations High Commissioner for Refugees has entrusted the spending of 2,900,000 dollars granted by the Ford Foundation in July 1952 for pilot projects intended to serve as models for schemes for the economic integration and assimilation of refugees, the training of young people, etc. The United Nations Relief and Works Agency for Palestine Refugees in the Near East (UNRWA) looked for Church help for the same reason; and the United Nations Korean Reconstruction Agency (UNKRA) invited the World Council to Korea, expecting to receive something from it. Such is the confidence which United Nations Agencies and officers repose in the World Council and its Service to Refugees.

12

ACTION FOR JUSTICE AND PEACE

WHEN the statesmen on the victorious side in the First World War were preparing for the Peace Conference at Versailles (1919), Charles Brent, Bishop of Western New York wrote to President Wilson making two requests. He urged first that the Conference should be opened with prayer; and secondly that some frank statement should be incorporated in the Covenant of the League, that mankind belonged to God and that we were set on working out his purpose. Both proposals failed. 'I need not tell you,' wrote President Wilson with regard to the latter, 'that the suggestion it [your letter] contains appeals to my heart, but I am afraid with the peculiar make-up of our Commission on the League of Nations it would be useless to propose such a sentence for the Covenant of the League.' A mere sentence, Bishop Brent commented at the Stockholm Conference (1935), 'is valueless unless it expresses a conviction under the jurisdiction of which we live. But the Christian Churches do live under the jurisdiction of that conviction, and it is their right and duty to state it to the world of nations'.

The World Council of Churches has a special duty to express such a conviction. The Amsterdam Assembly of 1948 expressed the following among other convictions with reference to international affairs:

The world in God's hands

The churches bear witness to all mankind that the world is in God's hands. His purpose may be thwarted and delayed, but it cannot be finally frustrated.

War a sin against God

War as a method of settling disputes is incompatible with the teaching and example of our Lord Jesus Christ. The part which war plays in our present international life is a sin against God and a degradation of man.

The State subject to God

Our Lord Jesus Christ taught that God, the Father of all, is Sovereign. We affirm, therefore, that no state may claim absolute sovereignty, or make laws without regard to the commandments of God and the welfare of mankind. It must accept its responsibility under the governance of God, and its subordination to law, within the society of nations.

At the same time, if the World Council is to give adequate expression to its convictions at a particular moment, any statement it makes must be addressed to a particular situation, and take account of the actual conditions. Hence the World Council would require the assistance of those with special knowledge of international affairs. As Sir Alfred Zimmern has written,

Firstly, there is a technique of politics. Caesar has a business of his own, which requires knowledge, training, skill, a special quality of judgement. Politics – and more especially international politics – require more than good will and fine aspirations. ... *Secondly*, the things of Caesar must be related to the things of God. Politics is not a closed department, any more than any other special activity.[1]

and again,

Between the things of Caesar and the Kingdom of God there is perpetual tension, a tension that is at its highest when, as in the case of Africa, Caesar's power is least subject to control. In order to play his part in Caesar's world, the Christian needs, on the one hand, to arm himself with an understanding of Caesar's problems – he must be able, so to speak, to out-Caesar Caesar on his own ground – and, on the other, the military metaphor may be excused, to keep open his line of communication with his own spiritual base.[2]

1. *Spiritual Values and World Affairs*, p. 7.
2. pp. 176–7.

It was in order to provide the World Council with the means of understanding Caesar's problems that the Commission of the Churches on International Affairs (C.C.I.A.) was formed in 1946, and made a joint permanent agency of the World Council of Churches and the International Missionary Council in 1948. The Commission consists of forty-five members, with Baron van Asbeck (Holland), Professor of International Law at the University of Leiden, as President, Sir Kenneth Grubb (Britain) as Chairman of the Executive Committee, and Dr O. Frederick Nolde (U.S.A.) as Director. The Commission of the Churches on International Affairs also has the assistance of 25 National Commissions, and 350 international correspondents.

A Technique of Politics

During the past six years the World Council of Churches has had to do with a good many particular subjects in the international field, and it looks to the Commission of the Churches on International Affairs for expert help. Some of the subjects are broad, and of general public interest. Others have a more specialist character. But as C.C.I.A. is the expert body dealing with general and particular situations and problems, it is important that it should be recognized as the instrument of the World Council (and the International Missionary Council) by inter-governmental organizations and by national governments. This applies not only to political, but also to economic questions, and to questions which have a wide social bearing.

Taking the first point in Zimmern's analysis, we must note that since the main contemporary forum for discussion and decisions on international problems is the United Nations, the Commission of the Churches on International Affairs must have a status with regard to that body. It has accordingly been registered with the United Nations Department of Public Information, which entitles it to have an observer at all open meetings of United Nations Organs, to receive documents, and obtain information and assistance. It has also been given a consultative relation with the United Nations Economic and Social Commission (Category B), and is therefore entitled to be represented by consultants, and to submit written statements and oral interventions. It has a similar consultative status with the United Nations Economic Social and Cultural Organization (UNESCO), 1949, and the Food and Agriculture Organization (FAO.), 1950.

Whenever the Assembly meets, Dr Nolde, or another member of the staff, is in attendance at the sessions, and makes careful preparations beforehand. Thus the transactions of past sessions are studied to discover 'unfinished business'; and consultations with delegates or secretariat reveal new issues to be considered. Over a period of three or four months preceding a General Assembly session the actions of the Churches and National Councils on particular topics are assembled, and broad resolutions are drafted for the consideration of the C.C.I.A. Executive Committee. When the provisional agenda of the General Assembly is issued, a special memorandum is prepared wherein the positions of the Churches are correlated with the items for United Nations debate and decision. This type of preparation paves the way for registering Christian views more effectively when the Assembly actually begins its session.

Further (and this applies not only to issues handled by the United Nations but to all issues involving Governments) the officers must show a practical realization of the nature of the particular problem involved. They must analyse that problem, in order to determine the facts by which it is characterized, and so that pertinent Christian truth may be interpreted in such a way that its relevance is clear, and its application seen to be politically possible. They must also realize that while statements by Church agencies may have general educational value, such statements have political effect only if their influence is felt at the time and place where decisions of international political importance are reached.

The Kingship of Christ

At the same time (taking Zimmern's second point) it must be remembered that, as Baron van Asbeck said when reporting to the World Council of Churches Central Committee at Rolle in 1951, the C.C.I.A. being an *ecumenical* Commission, 'must take a *supra*-national and not an *inter*-national view of affairs. It cannot identify itself with a State or a group of States, or with the United Nations, or with a political movement. It does not keep aloof from political affairs, but at every juncture must take a definite stand, not because it is the stand of a particular nation or group, but out of obedience to the will of God as revealed in the Bible, the book that speaks of the Justice of God in relation to world affairs. Therefore the prime target for the C.C.I.A. is the realization of justice.'

Further, while the purposes of the United Nations in the settlement of difficulties and the promotion of friendly relations among nations deserve the support of Christians, any idea that the United Nations is part of a Messianic scheme must be totally rejected. Obedience to the will of God is the Christian's spiritual base. It is the Kingship of Christ over the kingdoms of the world which is the supreme aim of the World Council of Churches.

Religious Liberty

There are certain major interests which stand out in the World Council's dealing in the field of international affairs.

From the very start the World Council has taken a particular interest in Religious Liberty and Human Rights. The resolutions on Religious Liberty adopted at Chichester (1949) and Toronto (1950) are evidence of the Council's attitude. It has interested itself consistently on behalf of religious minorities in different countries, partly through personal intervention, partly through statements published in the press. Ever since 1948 it has worked systematically for religious freedom all over the world. Its views, and through its officers the views of member Churches, are made known on particular points, or when a particular opening is given, such as the framing of a new Constitution for a people which has recently acquired independence.

Reference has been already made[1] to the two main paragraphs of the resolution adopted by the Central Committee at Toronto in 1950 on this general subject. The whole resolution was framed, and the discussion took place, on the basis of a comprehensive study drawn up by C.C.I.A. (by request) with the title 'Religious Freedom in face of Dominant Forces'. The Study is in three parts. *Part I:* (printed in the Toronto minutes) *The Defence of Religious Liberty* – an approach to a comprehensive plan for promoting the observance of religious freedom. *Part II: Supplementary data* – an assembly of selected information on areas where the problem of religious domination appears. *Part III: Papers submitted by Church leaders* indicating the nature and extent of the restriction upon religious freedom in the areas which they represent.

The Central Committee in the preamble to its resolution spoke of its attention having been called 'to serious infringements of religious freedom in certain countries in which the Roman Catholic faith is the dominant religion, and in regions in which the Muslim faith is the dominant religion', and also to reports 'concerning discrimination against

1. p. 86 [ch. 9].

religious minorities in countries where the Protestant or Orthodox Churches are dominant'. By way of conclusion it emphasized 'the vital importance of incorporating adequate safeguards of religious liberty within national Constitutions'; welcomed 'the recent enactment of such constitutional safeguards in various countries'; urged all Governments 'when drafting or amending Constitutions or laws to secure for all people within their jurisdictions the fundamental right of religious freedom'; and stressed 'the necessity of bringing local administration and practice into conformity with the law' when adequate standards have been enacted. These resolutions, and the report on which they were based, afford a charter both for watchfulness, and for action, on the part of all interested in the various Churches. It is not surprising that the assistance of the C.C.I.A. is being increasingly sought in situations where religious liberty has been threatened or violated, involving the seizure of Church property, the curtailment of freedom in pursuing normal Church activities, restrictions upon travel of missionaries and their admission to certain countries, and the imprisonment of missionaries. One of the most recent special issues taken up by the Commission arose out of grave reports of the persecution of Protestant Christians in Colombia.

Declaration of Human Rights

An illustration of the way in which the Commission brings its influence to bear on United Nations and the Human Rights Commission is to be found in a study of the steps which were involved in drafting an article on religious freedom in the Universal Declaration of Human Rights. The Director, Dr. Nolde, has described the process in a most effective way. First of all there was the action of the World Council of Churches and the International Missionary Council when it adopted a Declaration on Religious Liberty in which the basis for human rights was established in the nature and destiny of man by virtue of his creation, redemption, and calling. Next, different situations in many parts of the world had to be surveyed, so that the consequences of the Declaration might be expressed in a form which took account of the actual conditions. An analysis was then made of the particular ways in which the expression of religious freedom might take place. As a result the conclusion was reached that man should be able to manifest his religion or belief alone or in community with others, and in public or private. It was further concluded that worship, teaching, practice, and observance had all to be taken into account. Missionary needs indicated that a particular importance must be attached to freedom to *change* one's religion or belief. In the study by which these components of religious freedom were identified, Christian leaders from many parts of the world participated. Thus as a result of extensive study and investigation, the Churches were able to make a fairly precise representation, which flowed from their distinctive conviction and experience at the moment, to the whole discussion at United Nations Commissions where it was definitely relevant. The article which was finally incorporated in the Universal Declaration reads:

Everyone has the right to freedom of thought, conscience, and religion; this right includes freedom to change his religion or belief, and freedom, either alone or in community with others and in public or private, to manifest his religion or belief in teaching, practice, worship, and observance.

It will be noticed that freedom to change one's religion, as well as to manifest it in teaching, is secured. The Universal Declaration, including this article, was adopted and proclaimed by the United Nations General Assembly at Paris on 10 December 1948. The officers of C.C.I.A. have taken much trouble since then to call attention to the importance of the Declaration in the constituency of the World Council of Churches and the International Missionary Council. Thus on 6 November 1951, they wrote a special letter to the forty-five members of C.C.I.A. and to the National Church Commissions, and selected correspondents, calling their attention to the opportunities which the anniversary of the Declaration afforded. According to the reports received, this action was particularly helpful in countries where religious freedom was locally threatened or restricted.

The Commission has continued in active contact with the Human Rights Commission of the United Nations in the work it is doing on two further Covenants on Human Rights, one dealing with civil and political, the other with economic, social, and cultural rights.

Times of International Tension

The Officers of the World Council and the Commission of the Churches on International Affairs are naturally alive to the duty of churchmen to be particularly on the watch for opportunities of service in times of grave international tension. The status of C.C.I.A. in relation to the United Nations and to the Governments with which the Officers are in special touch gives them a means of securing information and exchanging reflections which is of special value. Further, the development of the World Council as an ecumenical reality in a divided world is an important factor in relation to the East-West division. The World Council maintains regular contacts with a number of Churches in Eastern Europe. Representatives of those Churches are present at meetings of the Central Committee; and the frank discussion at their meetings and the experience of unity shown by the delegates demonstrate how the Churches find bonds with one another after a fashion that overcomes political divisions. A similar sense of the support of their brethren in the World Council meant much to the churchmen in East Germany at the time of the new attacks which were made by the State on the Church and its youth movement in the spring of 1953, and ceased in June.

Peace Observers

The action taken by the World Council on different occasions in connexion with the Korean War has already been described. The reference to the value of an umpire in the chairman's letter addressed from Lucknow to the President of the United Nations Assembly[1] will be remembered. It is of interest also in connexion with the Korean War to note action taken as a result of C.C.I.A. intervention in favour of setting up peace observers.

In August 1950, that is shortly after the outbreak of the Korean war, the C.C.I.A. officers made a proposal that consideration be given to the establishment of a 'widespread system of United Nations Observer Commissions' to deter aggression or to identify aggressors, and this was supported by leading churchmen in representations to several Governments in the United Nations. The main elements of the proposal were subsequently incorporated in the *Uniting for Peace* resolution approved overwhelmingly by the United Nations General Assembly on 3 November 1950. At its Sixth Session in 1951, the General Assembly requested the Peace Observation Commission to establish a Balkan sub-commission because of the tense situation in that area; and on 23 January 1952 it was established for the current year with the following members: Colombia, France, Pakistan, Sweden, and U.S.A.

Underdeveloped Regions

There are many other fields in relation to the United Nations in which the services of the Commission of the

1. p. 96.

Churches on International Affairs have been and are of great value. Particular importance is likely to be attached in the near future to its contacts with the Social and Economic commission. It is taking a special interest in the technical assistance programmes and also in expressing Christian concerns in regard to food and agriculture. In this, it gives witness to the Churches' deep concern and respect for the rights and welfare of the people in the underdeveloped regions. It also shows a lively interest in the work of the United Nations Trusteeship Council.

Atomic Weapons

The Executive of the Central Committee met in February 1950, immediately after President Truman's instruction to the U.S. Atomic Energy Commission on 31 January 1950 to continue work on all atomic weapons including the hydrogen bomb. And since peace is in a particular way the interest of the Churches and in view of the alarming development of modern methods of war, I propose to devote the rest of this chapter to a consideration of the World Council's attitude to atom bombs and similar weapons and to a description of the attitude it has adopted in relation to peace appeals.

The Executive Committee denounced the hydrogen bomb as 'the latest and most terrible step in the crescendo of warfare which has changed war from a fight between men and nations to a mass murder of human life' It added:

All men have responsibilities before God as they face the grave issues raised by the hydrogen bomb and other weapons of modern war. . . . The governments of the nations have an inescapable responsibility at this hour. The world is divided into hostile camps through suspicion and distrust, and through the failure of the nations to bring their mutual relations within an agreed system of justice and order. As representatives of Christian Churches we appeal for a gigantic new effort for peace.

The Stockholm Appeal

A first Peace Congress under Communist auspices had been held in Paris in April 1949. The Paris Congress set up a permanent World Committee of Partisans of Peace, later known as the World Peace Committee. The World Peace Committee (after its first plenary meeting in Rome in October 1949) held its second plenary meeting in Stockholm in March 1950. It issued an appeal known as the 'Stockholm Appeal'. It reads as follows:

We demand the total banning of the atomic weapon, the arm of terror and the mass extermination of populations.

We demand the establishment of strict international control to ensure the implementation of the ban.

We consider that any Government which first uses the atomic weapon against any country whatsoever would be committing a crime against humanity and should be dealt with as a war criminal.

We call on all men of good will to sign this appeal.

When the Central Committee of the World Council met in Toronto in July 1950, it made a statement on the Korean situation and World Order which included the following paragraph:

Such methods of modern warfare as the use of atomic and bacteriological weapons and obliteration bombing involve force and destruction of life on so terrible a scale as to imperil the very basis on which law and civilization can exist. It is, therefore, imperative that they should be banned by international agreement and we welcome every sincere proposal to this end. However, the 'Stockholm Appeal', which demands the outlawing of atomic weapons only, without effective international inspection and control, both immediate and continuous, must be regarded as a strategy of propaganda rather than a genuine peace proposal. We must seek peace by cultivating mutual confidence and work for an increasing devotion to common moral principles.

At the same time, the officers of the C.C.I.A. issued a letter to their colleagues in different countries in which they

pointed out serious differences between the principles underlying the Stockholm Appeal and those which are held by
Christians. They also pointed out that the term 'Strict
international control' is the term already used by Soviet
representatives to describe their proposal for *national* owner-
ship and management, *periodic* (as against continuous) inspection of declared facilities, and *special* investigations when
suspicions of violations arise. The purposes of the Comin-
form campaign may be manifold, but there is no indication
that a fresh start in the Atomic negotiations is among them.

Approach by the World Peace Council

In January 1951, M. Joliot-Curie, President of the World
Peace Council, made a direct approach to the Presidents of
the World Council of Churches asking for the Council's
support for the appeal made by the 'Second World Congress
of the Defenders of Peace' (in succession to the Stockholm
Appeal), that all kinds of atomic, bacteriological, chemical,
toxic, and radio-active weapons, and all other means of
mass-destruction, be entirely prohibited; and that during
1951–2 there should be a gradual reduction simultaneously
and in the same proportion of all armed land, sea, and air
forces, this reduction being increased from one-third to a
half.

The Presidents entrusted the task of replying to the officers
of C.C.I.A. In February 1951 these officers, writing to
M. Joliot-Curie, informed him of various statements made
by the World Council through its organs on the subject of disarmament, and emphasized the importance of an adequate
international combined force of United Nations, organized
to safeguard any State against aggression of any kind, and
to enforce international law.

In June 1951, M. Joliot-Curie wrote again to the Presidents calling their attention to the World Peace Council's

new campaign for a peace pact among the five great Powers.

These various proposals came before the Central Committee and the Commission of the Churches on International Affairs at Rolle in Switzerland in August 1951. The Central Committee adopted a statement by its Executive Committee in which it gave its reasons for declining to join in issuing a general appeal for peace, including the following paragraph:

All the members of the Executive Committee, as indeed all the Churches represented on the World Council of Churches loathe war. They realize to the full the ruinous consequences with which the world is threatened should war break out. They therefore believe that the utmost efforts should be made at every point possible to prevent war starting, and that, as such efforts are made persistently and sincerely, their cumulative effect in promoting peace will be great. But peace is not a magic condition which can be conjured up by a stroke of the pen. The present acute international tension has lasted too long, and is too complex in origin, to admit of a quick termination, or a simple solution. Nor are they true friends of peace who, while crying out for peace, create strife and so intensify division.

The Central Committee did not consider the issuing of a general peace appeal 'a practicable policy or one that would help the general situation', but instructed its Executive Committee and the C.C.I.A. 'to watch for opportunities of co-operation on concrete issues where there was some promise of a fruitful intervention on just grounds'. The C.C.I.A. Executive Committee at the same time issued the following brief formulation of principles for the guidance of Christians:

CHRISTIANS STAND FOR PEACE

1. As Christians it is our duty to seek both peace and justice. We no less than others detest war and we shall do everything in our power to prevent present tensions and limited conflicts from leading to a third world war. Yet we must neither purchase peace at the price of tyranny nor in the name of justice look on war as a way to justice or as a ground of hope.

2. We stand opposed to every form of oppression and aggression. We condemn any extension of oppression, carried on behind a

façade of propaganda for peace. We condemn equally the proposal of a preventive war, or the use for aggressive purposes of atomic weapons.

3. We do not believe that peace will come merely by new pacts or disarmament. There must first be a sufficient mutual trust and good faith between nations to ensure that agreements will be honoured. Peace and disarmament will follow from mutual trust; they will not automatically create it.

4. In present world conditions peace and justice require international organs of law and order. We therefore fully support all forms of co-operation between the nations which will serve this purpose. Believing that the United Nations and its agencies present now the best means to develop the rule of law over the nations, we condemn unilateral military action in defiance of decisions under the Charter of the United Nations.

5. We press urgently for the most generous assistance by the wealthier to the poorer nations of the world in their economic and social development, and for the immediate sharing by all nations in responsibility for the millions of refugees.

6. We believe that it is the duty of all Governments and of the United Nations to recognize the dignity of man as a child of God, and to protect the right of the individual. Every denial of fundamental rights should be made known and resisted.

7. Christians can witness convincingly to peace only if they and their Churches, in their relations with one another across all frontiers, put loyalty to their common Lord above any other loyalty.

On 9 August after the discussion in the Central Committee the officers of the Commission of the Churches on International Affairs wrote to M. Joliot-Curie saying that they were ready to discuss the various matters raised informally and privately with representatives of the World Peace Council. This offer was welcomed, and, as a result, a conference was held in Paris on 24 November 1951, between M. Joliot-Curie and three of his colleagues, and Baron van Asbeck and four colleagues. The following agreed *communiqué* was issued after the meeting:

They [the representatives present] proceeded to an exchange of information and a clarification of their respective positions on the leading international problems and on their respective modes of approaching these in the total setting of the problem of peace and justice.

They examined more particularly the disarmament question, that of the control of atomic weapons and of all weapons of war, that of the peaceful coexistence of different political and social regimes, and other questions such as the importance which must be attributed for the maintenance of peace to the protection of human rights and to technical assistance for underdeveloped areas.

They decided to proceed to the exchange of documents and they will consider the advisability of meeting again.

Dr Nolde, in commenting on the meeting, stated that it had made clear that there are vital differences between the basic conceptions and the approaches of the two bodies concerned with the problems of peace. However, the discussion had offered an opportunity for the removal of misunderstanding.

No further discussions have taken place. But it should be added that the World Council of Churches and C.C.I.A. are deeply concerned about the need of an agreed plan for disarmament under international control, for the banning of the hydrogen bomb and similar weapons, and for a just settlement of outstanding issues between the Powers. Nor is there any weakening in their conviction that a positive attempt must be made to ensure that competing economic systems, such as Communism, Socialism, and free enterprise, may coexist without leading to war.

13

THE RACE QUESTION

AMONG all the questions confronting the world at the present time the race question is pre-eminent. As 'a fellowship of Churches' within which all the races of mankind are represented, and as a body the very *raison d'être* of which is to render witness to the unity and universality of the Church of Christ, the World Council is bound to be concerned with the relationship between races.

Since the Assembly at Amsterdam asked the Churches to take a firm and vigorous stand against discrimination or segregation on grounds of race and colour, the question of enforced segregation has been raised in an acute form in South Africa. Attention was called to the policy of *apartheid* at the meeting of the Central Committee at Chichester in 1949, by Bishop Walls, of the African Methodist Episcopal Zion Church, U.S.A. On his representation, it was agreed that the Commission of the Churches on International Affairs should be instructed to study racial questions with particular reference to South Africa. The study was undertaken, and a member of the World Council secretariat paid a special visit to South Africa. This was followed by a full debate in the Central Committee at Toronto in July 1950. The position was described as seen from the points of view of both White and Black. Mr Marais, a minister of the Dutch Reformed Church, described conditions in South Africa, and spoke of the reasons behind *apartheid*. Dr Benjamin Mays, President of Morehouse College, Atlanta, Georgia, spoke of the rights of the 8,000,000 Bantus in South Africa.

The question was, how could the Central Committee help

towards a solution of the problem? There was general agreement that far the best step would be by means of a delegation for the purposes of conference and fellowship with the Churches of South Africa. It was also quite clear that any delegation which called itself 'ecumenical' must be multi-racial. The Central Committee therefore resolved to let the Churches in South Africa know of its willingness to send such a delegation, if those Churches were ready to receive it. When news of the resolution was received in South Africa, there was a division of opinion. The Afrikaans-speaking Churches replied that they did not desire to receive such a delegation. The English-speaking Churches stated that the principle of such a delegation was acceptable to them, but that the plan did not seem to be practicable at the present time. No delegation could therefore be sent. But at the next meeting of the Central Committee in Switzerland, in August 1951, the hope was expressed that Dr Visser 't Hooft would be able to visit South Africa during 1952. It was felt that this would enable the character of the World Council to be explained to the Churches there, on points where explanation was necessary, and also provide opportunity for conference and fellowship on the race question.

Visit to South Africa

As a result Dr Visser 't Hooft paid a six weeks' visit to South Africa in April and May 1952. He visited all the four Provinces, as well as Basutoland; met representatives of the main sections of South African life, political, industrial, educational; and talked with African and coloured ministers as well as European. His report, published in the *Ecumenical Review* of January 1953, is a masterly document. It shows a remarkable appreciation of the many angles from which the total situation may be approached; and it is quite clear that both his understanding of the human and political aspects, and his theological grasp, exercised a deep influence. He reported fully to the Central Committee at Lucknow in January 1953. He emphasized the rare opportunity which he had as an ecumenical visitor, with doors open to him that were not open to any living inside South Africa. He also laid special emphasis on the serious consequences for Africans of the impact of modern technical society upon simple, rural, collectivist communities without adequate attempts for the conservation of human values.

There was a vigorous discussion, in which not only Bishop Walls and Dr Mays, but also Raja Maharaj Singh and others in India and Burma, spoke of the need of the World Council standing four-square on the fact that there is no Christian foundation for a colour bar; and insisted that the situation admitted of no delay. A series of resolutions was passed, welcoming the commencement of a constructive conversation between South African member Churches and the World Council on this subject, and emphasizing the point that the foremost contribution which the Churches could and must make to the solution of the race problem was to manifest in their own lives that in Christ all racial divisions are overcome; and that a policy of enforced segregation in any aspects of Church life was incompatible with the very nature of the Church. Emphasis was also laid on the desirability of asking representative non-European Christians in South Africa to share in the deliberations on the race question. The Central Committee considered that the full participation of the South African Churches in the Commission on inter-group relations, set up in preparation for the Assembly at Evanston, was essential.

It should be added that the Afrikaans- and English-speaking Churches held an important conference on the race question in Pretoria 17–19 November 1953, in which there was very frank discussion, and that they are planning a further conference together with the Bantu Churches.

Active discussions are proceeding in many places in different continents on the whole subject of Christianity and the race problem, which will form one of the main subjects for discussion at the Evanston Assembly.

14

MISSION AND UNITY

BISHOP AZARIAH of Dornakal (India) was asked to speak at the Edinburgh Conference of 1937 on the Church's Witness to the World Today. He had been the outstanding champion of Church union in South India ever since 1919. I remember him vividly at the Lambeth Conference of 1920, where I first saw him, a very young Bishop in a purple cassock, with his black hair, sparkling eyes, and eager speech, appealing to his elder brothers in the Anglican communion to give their support to the formation of a united Church in South India, of which four Anglican dioceses would be a large part. It was another twenty-eight years before union came.

He told the Edinburgh audience of a conversation with Dr Ambedkar, the leader of the Untouchables, in 1935. It was after the latter's denunciation of the caste system; when he called upon his 60,000,000 fellow Untouchables to renounce Hinduism with him. They had to find another religion than Hinduism. Many of them, Dr Ambedkar said, are much drawn to the acceptance of Jesus Christ as the Way, the Truth, and the Life: but 'when Christianity is mentioned, they remind me of the many divisions within the Christian Church. We are united in Hinduism, say they, and we shall become divided in Christianity'. And Bishop Azariah could only confess – 'I had no answer to give'. The Bishop ended his speech a few minutes later with these words: 'We want you to take us seriously when we say that the problem of union is one of life and death with us'.

The same kind of appeal is constantly made whenever representatives of the younger Churches meet their parents. They do not understand why the Churches of the West were so late in coming to their lands, or why they bring their divisions with them! Nor, if it comes to that, why an Anglican in England is more excited about Archimandrites in Bulgaria than about the Congregationalist next door, when, after all, the Christians in a country have to do together what God has intended that they shall do together.

Parent Churches and younger Churches alike are involved in a missionary situation. The character of the challenge varies from culture to culture and from country to country: but in essence it is the same. All Christians are called to proclaim the Kingship of Christ. But, as Dr Charles Ranson, General Secretary of the International Missionary Council, puts it, 'Wherever the Church recognizes itself as standing in a missionary situation, the question of unity becomes vital. The complacency of the Churches concerning their disunity can only be accounted for by the loss of the conviction that the Church exists to fulfil a mission. It was not an accident that the foundations of the modern ecumenical movement, with its concern for Christian unity, were laid by the organized missionary enterprise'.[1]

The realization of this truth has important implications for the life of the Church. For example, every congregation of whatever denomination, or in whatever country, ought to regard its obligation to proclaim the Kingship of Christ to its own neighbourhood and to the whole world as the first priority. Every congregation awake to this mission is bound to face the issue of unity. The approach to unity takes different forms. But if there is any conviction at all about the urgency of the missionary call, there must be some kind of fellowship with other congregations. Every theological college ought to regard the teaching of this missionary obligation to the future ministers of its Church as a primary task. Every theological college is therefore

1. C. W. Ranson, *That the World may Know* (Friendship Press, New York, 1953), p. 123.

also bound to bring the issue of unity home to its students, and to help them to see that the call to Church union is a paramount call.

The realization of the truth of the close interconnexion of 'mission' and 'unity' has important implications also for the world missionary task. For example the older Churches ought not to confuse the unchanging Gospel with the particular cultural, economic, and institutional forms in which they have grown up. The older Churches should not be parties to the creation of Churches which are foreign to the country in which they exist. Too often the very names of Churches bear the impress of their Western origin. 'Are you an Indian Christian?' asked William Paton, travelling in India, of a young man on the platform selling copies of the Gospels. 'No, sir. I am a Canadian Baptist,' was the disconcerting reply! The older Churches should give freedom to the younger Churches to express their Christian obedience in new forms, under the guidance of the Holy Spirit. They must also be willing to share the vision of the younger Churches for their own enrichment.

The International Missionary Council

There is another field in which the intimate connexion of Mission and Unity carries consequences for the World Council of Churches itself. Since the future relation of Mission and Unity on a world scale is of great importance, we ought now to consider how the World Council itself stands in relation to the International Missionary Council, a parallel but older body, which deals with missionary problems as such.

The International Missionary Council (as already observed) sprang directly out of the Conference at Edinburgh in 1910. This Conference appointed a 'Continuation Committee' which in 1922 was given new shape as the International Missionary Council. It is a Council of councils. Some of the member councils are National Missionary Councils, composed of representatives of the older Missionary Societies or parent Churches. Others are National Christian Councils, composed of representatives of the younger Churches, especially in Asia and Africa and parts of South America. The International Missionary Council is specially concerned with work on the frontiers of the Churches' action, where Christianity is in direct conflict with other religions or with paganism. Among its functions are

(a) To strengthen its member organizations throughout the world in the service of their Churches and missionary organizations and in the active encouragement of evangelism.

(b) To stimulate thinking and investigation on questions directly related to the mission and expansion of Christianity in the world. . . .

(c) To help to co-ordinate the activities of its member organizations. . . .

(d) To seek to unite Christian public opinion and to act as required in support of freedom of conscience and of religion, including liberty of worship, the right to educate and persuade, and the right to change religious allegiance.

(e) To help to unite the Christian forces of the world in seeking justice in international and inter-racial relations.

The World Council of Churches

The World Council is a Council of Churches. It includes member Churches in the East and the West, both older and younger. It is in the main the creation of the Churches of the historic traditions, belonging to countries where the Christian faith has been established for a considerable time. Its two founding bodies, Life and Work and Faith and Order, had very few representatives of the younger Churches. The International Missionary Council, however, came into direct connexion with Life and Work on the express proposal of William Paton, the Secretary of the International Missionary Council, at the Fäno meeting of the Universal Christian Council for Life and Work in 1934. He proposed, and it was agreed, 'that its National Councils for Asia and Africa should be accepted as doing the work of the Fifth Section of the Universal Christian Council'. (The Fifth Section represented the Churches of Other Lands, the other four Sections being Orthodox, Continental European, British, and American.) It was pointed out that since these Churches were related to .the International Missionary Council, this arrangement would obviate duplication that might occur if they were related separately to the Universal Christian Council. It would also 'ensure that the younger Churches were adequately and valuably represented at ecumenical meetings through the I.M.C., which would do everything possible to secure the right people and to follow up such representation afterwards in the Churches concerned'.

Present Links

We have to recognize, however, as a matter of history that the International Missionary Council and the World Council have developed as two distinct organizations. These two organizations also represent somewhat different constituencies, and gather to themselves different enthusiasms. It has often been suggested that, while among non-Roman Churches the nineteenth century was the great 'missionary century', the twentieth century bids fair to be called the 'ecumenical century'. But such a division in thought or action would be treason to the whole conception of the Church. It is not only that 'missionary' and 'ecumenical' are complementary to one another: they must be united. The obligation to take the Gospel to the whole world, and the obligation to draw all Christ's people together, both rest upon Christ's whole work, and are indissolubly connected. Every attempt to separate these two tasks violates the wholeness of Christ's ministry to the world. Both of them are, in the strict sense of the word, essential to the being of the Church and the fulfilment of its function as the Body of Christ.

The first formal step for establishing a relationship between them was taken in 1948, when it was agreed that the words 'in association with the International Missionary Council' should be part of the general description of the World Council of Churches; and *vice versa*. It was also agreed to continue the existing Joint Committee of the two bodies, with its own Chairman, for the purpose of dealing with all questions with regard to collaboration between the two bodies. Further steps have been taken to secure more and more effective collaboration. Thus the international field is one of the most obviously important fields in which close collaboration between the two bodies is essential. An earlier chapter shows the wide range of ground common to both which the Churches' Commission on International Affairs covers, not only in relation to religious liberty, and other matters of great importance in the sphere of missions and Governments, but also in relation to bringing about conditions generally more favourable to the world-wide proclamation of the Gospel. It was only natural and right, therefore, that the Commission of the Churches on International Affairs should have been immediately recognized in 1948 by the Amsterdam Assembly and the International Missionary Council as the permanent agency of both bodies, each sharing responsibility for its support.

The Younger Churches

Again, if the younger Churches are to be brought into increasingly closer personal relations both with one another and with member Churches in the West, it is most desirable that a particular officer, living in East Asia and in close contact with the officers of the International Missionary Council and the World Council of Churches in Europe and America, should be appointed as personal ambassador for both bodies. His duty would be to visit the younger Churches in East Asia and keep them in constant touch with the activities of all the Churches and missions, and with the headquarters of both bodies. The value of a possible office of the International Missionary Council in East Asia had been recognized as far back as the World Missionary Conference at Tambaram, near Madras, in 1938. The proposal that there should be a joint office was approved in principle in 1947; and when the first East Asian Christian Conference was held at Bangkok in 1949, it was eagerly welcomed. Dr Rajah Manikam, a well-known Indian Christian, Executive Secretary of the Christian Council of India and Pakistan, who had been chairman of the Bangkok Conference, was appointed in 1950 Joint Secretary for East Asia. The Christians in East Asia are a tiny minority in the midst of some 1,160,000,000 people, more than half the entire population of the world. The several Churches in East Asia have hitherto been in touch with their several parent Churches in the West, but seldom with one another. Dr Manikam's appointment is of peculiar importance in the development of mutual knowledge, and the sense of interdependence of the younger Churches. He has already paid visits to a great number of these Churches, and opened many new doors in the ecumenical movement.

Once more, there is the tremendous problem of how member Churches in Asia and Africa can best cope with grave emergencies arising out of war or pestilence or famine and the like. The World Council of Churches has a well-tried department of Inter-Church Aid and Service to Refugees. It again seemed the natural and proper course that the responsibilities of this department, by agreement between the International Missionary Council and the World Council, should be extended from countries within Europe to meeting emergencies occasioned by natural disasters, war, or civil strife in countries outside Europe; and also to 'relief' in the sense of a response, so far as is practicable, to general distress in any country or area. This has led to the large volume of relief work in Korea, and the work among Arab refugees in Palestine, which has been already described.

Further, there are great world needs calling for Christian service. Wherever the Gospel is preached, the Churches, the Christian Councils, and the Missionary Societies have some responsibility with regard to the conditions of the populations amongst whom their missionaries live. By its Charter United Nations is pledged 'to promote social progress and better standards of life in larger freedom'. For this purpose it has undertaken programmes of technical assistance for underdeveloped countries. Some of the great Powers are engaged in similar plans. Extreme inequalities of wealth between different areas are a challenge to the Christian conscience. It may well be that, in a world in which hunger and destitution are the lot of so many millions of our fellow human beings, increasing as the population increases, the principal call to the richer countries in the immediate future will be to rescue them from misery, and to do justice to their needs. But if any action on the part of the Churches and Christian missions is to be effective on a world scale, the fullest collaboration between them is essential on a world scale. Hence the call to the World Council and the International Missionary Council to consider together the opportunities which the new programmes of technical assistance suggest; and to do their best together to develop the activities and finances both of the Churches' Commission on International Affairs and of the Department of Inter-Church Aid.

There are other matters, especially on the side of study, in which the International Missionary Council and the World Council can come closer together. The Churches in

Asia and Africa have much fewer resources in personnel, theological equipment, educational technique; they have far less access to the discoveries of modern science, or the developments of modern philosophy; and far fewer opportunities for research, or for comparing their knowledge with that of others working in the same field. It was because of their almost overwhelming awareness of this fact that the representatives of these Churches and of the National Christian Councils of Asia, meeting at Lucknow in December 1952, at an Ecumenical Study Conference for East Asia, pressed very hard for the necessity of the complete integration of the World Council and the International Missionary Council study programmes, if effective ecumenical study is to be secured.

The Future

But the principal question still remains: Is it possible for the World Council of Churches and the International Missionary Council to form, within the next few years, a single Council? Can such a single Council, if created, be trusted to take proper care of all those institutions and issues which have been the responsibility of the International Missionary Council ever since its formation? Is it essential to the very idea of Mission that it *must* be free in the last resort from all ecclesiastical organization? And there is this question of principle: does the concept of Church demand that in the last resort the Church must be the guiding force behind missionary effort, or die?

There are many ways, no doubt, in which the question may be put and many forms which the answer may take. But let us, for the sake of argument, assume that the answer is, 'Yes, in the last resort the Church must be the guiding force behind missionary effort'. In what constitutional way could effect be given to this working-out in practice?

We face first the problem of the Councils of which the International Missionary Council is composed, and their place in relation to a Council of Churches. Its solution is not too difficult. It would actually be in line with the proposed development in structure of the World Council itself, to give the Councils full consultative status, and opportunities for mutual consultation. But it is at the centre of the organization that the biggest problem arises. At the moment it appears that the Joint Committee may be further strengthened, as advisory to both, and provided with its own secretariat. But a lasting solution has yet to be found, bringing both bodies under one roof, with full justice being done to missionary enthusiasm and initiative.

Here is a purely tentative and unofficial proposal, derived in part from the experience gained in securing for Faith and Order its fundamental place on the World Council of Churches by means of a Faith and Order Commission. The proposal is that a special Commission should be appointed under Article VI of the Constitution of the World Council, and that this Commission should be charged with the care of the traditional concerns and responsibilities of the International Missionary Council. It might be called the 'International Missionary Commission' (so keeping very close to the present title), or, if preferred, 'The Commission on the World Mission of the Church'. It would have its own separate Constitution, and be as fully responsible for all matters hitherto cared for by the International Missionary Council as the Faith and Order Commission is for all matters previously cared for by the Faith and Order movement. It would be a Commission with its own membership, composed of persons appointed by the Assembly (or the Central Committee) in the light of recommendations made by the Commission itself. It would require a good deal of working out; and many objections would no doubt have to be met. But it is one way of securing the 'single council'.

15

STUDY THE BASIS OF ACTION:
THE LAYMAN

At a weekend Conference of philosophers and political thinkers from Britain and the Continent, held at Chichester in February 1935, I was brought up sharp against the differences between Continental and British scholars. It was the first research group meeting since the decision reached at Fäno to hold the Oxford Conference on Church, Community, and State. Here were made the first contributions to the question of the Christian understanding of man, of history, and of the common life, in order to map out the necessary line of approach and draft proposals for further study from an ecumenical viewpoint. To most of the British participants the Germans and the Swedes were strangers. They could at first find no common ground. The British were so 'practical', and the others so full of theory. 'Well,' said one of the British members – a famous Professor of Political Science at Cambridge at the end of the first session – 'these Continentals have a theology of the catacombs!' But, had his colleague from Germany heard him make that remark, he would almost certainly have said 'these British have no theology at all!' As the weekend proceeded, however, the British and the Continentals got together and commenced a study related to an actual situation, which proved very fruitful for the common task.

Church, Community, and State

I mention this incident as a modest illustration not so much of the different angles from which Anglo-Saxons and many

Continentals approach a particular subject, but of the valuable results of a common study of the problems of contemporary society on an ecumenical level. It so happens that Dr J. H. Oldham, the main architect of the Oxford Conference, was the leader in this discussion. There can be few men to whom the Ecumenical movement owes more than it owes to him, for his leadership in thinking, and for his insistence on the indispensable role which study, systematically pursued in collaboration with a definite purpose, must play in the life of the Church if the witness of the Church is to be relevant. Dr Hans Schonfeld (Germany), Director of the Life and Work Research Department, also took part. He deserves a special tribute for his service during long years, before his health gave way as the result of the strain imposed on him by his loyalty alike to the ecumenical movement in Geneva, and to the resistance movement in Germany.

It was at the meeting in Chichester (at which the present Director of the Study Department, Nils Ehrenstrom (Sweden), was present as a very young man) that the programme of work for the whole theme of Church, Community and State was outlined for the first time. The experience which followed, up to and including the Oxford Conference, made it unalterably clear that without study the ecumenical movement would be only half alive; and that therefore a Study Department, as good and well staffed as it could secure, was vital to the World Council of Churches.

The Study Department and the Churches

The Study Department was responsible for the preparation of the subjects of the four Sections at Amsterdam, under the leadership of Dr Henry P. van Dusen (President of the Union Theological Seminary, New York). The Amsterdam Assembly gave it a new charter, by which its activities have been governed since 1948. In the report presented by Dr

Ehrenstrom to the Central Committee at Toronto, it is pointed out that the formation of the World Council at Amsterdam has created a new situation for the Study Department, making it an enterprise *by* the Churches and *for* the Churches. Instead of concentrating on what the Department may be able to achieve under its own direct auspices, primary emphasis is laid on what the Churches, their relevant agencies and other groups can be persuaded to do over the years – and do better than before. What is envisaged is ecumenical 'fermentation', and not in the first place the production of more ecumenical literature. Many groups, especially such as are engaged in new experiments in evangelism, have put it as a condition of their co-operation that no public attention should be drawn to their endeavours, and no findings expected for international circulation until after some years. Such an approach, not yielding quick results, is likely to make a more abiding impact on the life and thought of the Churches than more spectacular methods.

It is an essential element in this policy that no rigid scheme be imposed from above. Great flexibility is maintained. The Department approaches groups or agencies engaged on some particular subject within its programme, enjoins them to pursue their work with a wider ecumenical perspective, and seeks to establish channels of communication between those concerned with the same kind of problems. Where there are no local or national initiatives which seem to be a suitable 'grafting spot' for an ecumenical project, steps are taken to form *ad hoc* groups. Throughout, the purpose is not study for the sake of study, but work for the renewal and advance of the Church. Under this policy the chief function of the Department is the definition of issues in the Church for study, stimulation and co-ordination, directed exchange, and occasional summing up of results. In sum, the aim is to promote – through a concerted attack on concrete problems – the organic growth of an ecumenical mind within the Churches.

There is, however, a serious difficulty about this new approach when there is a lack of co-operation in the member Churches. One of the functions of the World Council is 'to promote co-operation in study'. But (says a later report) 'it is an undeniable fact that the member Churches on the whole still show a disquieting apathy and unconcern as regards this aspect of their common enterprise'. All the greater, therefore, is the need of a maximum both of theological study and of the power to infect others in many Churches with a zest for the encounter of minds. All the more important is it that those in charge of the Study Department should both select those issues which are really fundamental to the Church and society today, and should get a 'fermentation' started in as many Churches as it can reach.

Major Inquiries

Besides serving as a centre of information on developments in religious thought and Church life, the Study Department has concentrated on three major inquiries since Amsterdam:

1. *The Bible and the Church's Message to the World*. Although the Bible as a matter of course is acknowledged as *the* basic ecumenical record, it is a curious fact that only slight attempts have thus far been made to elucidate its ecumenical message and to establish its relevance for the conversation between the Churches. Thus the inquiry which the Department has been carrying on for several years on 'The Biblical Authority for the Church's Social and Political Message Today' represents a new departure. Part of its results have been summed up in a symposium containing nineteen contributions from all major denominations and areas of the

World Council constituency.[1] It explains the authority of the Bible according to different traditions, discusses guiding principles of interpretation and application, and outlines from an ecumenical perspective the biblical message on such subjects as nation, state, and property.

2. *The Evangelization of Man in Modern Mass Society*. The significance of this inquiry is beyond dispute. The penetration of the Gospel into the alien world of industrialized mass society is one of the most urgent and most baffling tasks confronting the Church today. This inquiry is thus a challenge to the Churches to re-examine their evangelistic strategy and to strike out on new, unconventional trails. In such a vast field, pilot projects and experiments which set a new pattern are of far greater value than general theoretical statements. Emphasis has therefore been laid on encouraging or instigating local experiments of varied kinds, and arranging for their critical evaluation. Particular care has therefore to be taken to look out for new forms of Christian community life within a mass society; and to relate all such enterprises to a sound theology of evangelism. More than this, one of the greatest of the Church's problems today is the problem of communication, how to find a way to bridge the enormous gap which separates Biblical and other acceptable forms of theological statement at the present day from the habitual modes of expression of the city dweller of the twentieth century, whose mind is coloured through and through with the broad concepts and methods of the natural sciences.

3. *Christian Action in Society*. The initial aim of this study has been to define with more detail and precision the characteristics of *A Responsible Society* which Christians of the most diverse political and economic allegiances can support. Two tasks are involved. There is the task of furnish-

1. *Biblical Authority for Today* edited by A. Richardson and W. Schweitzer – S.C.M.

ing standards by which all existing and projected systems may be measured. There is also the task of dealing with the concrete situations which confront great numbers of individual Christians at their jobs within present-day secular society, as artisans or managers, employers or labour leaders or professional men and women.

The Study Department has during the past three years been very closely engaged in study preparations for the Second Assembly of the World Council at Evanston. The Main Theme, 'Christ the Hope of the World', has been entrusted to an Advisory Commission of some thirty theologians and laymen of different nations and Churches in the East and the West. The six subsidiary topics, including (2) and (3) above, have also been the subject of introductory leaflets, descriptive surveys, and draft reports, all prepared by the Study Department. Indeed the preparations for Evanston have enlisted a co-operation from the Churches on a world scale unprecedented in any previous ecumenical enterprise.

The Ecumenical Institute

One of the most remarkable embodiments of the ecumenical movement is the Ecumenical Institute at the Château de Bossey, twelve miles from Geneva. It is a place where all the things for which the World Council stands are expounded, discussed, and lived. In beautiful surroundings, within a mile of the shores of the Lake, and with a chapel of its own, it provides accommodation for some eighty guests, courses for study, and an atmosphere of conference and worship. The Director is Dr Hendrik Kraemer, of Holland. The main purpose of the Institute is to be a training centre for the laity of different countries and Churches, and to help the layman to give witness to his faith in his own occupation, and in the perplexities of the actual situation of the modern world.

'Since the Christian Church can face the troubled world of today only by the witness of a spiritually intelligent and active laity', Dr Kraemer writes in his introduction to *Contributions to a Christian Social Ethic* (one of the papers of the Ecumenical Institute), 'it is essential for the Church resolutely to tackle this problem. The laity, generally speaking, feels itself spiritually powerless and illiterate as to its witness in its professional life, that is in the very place where most of its life is spent. To alter this would mean a colossal change for the Church, both in her interior life and in her relations with the world outside. It is only through her lay members that the Church can live *in* the world without becoming *of* the world'.

The opening of the Institute and the purchase and reconstruction of the building were made possible by two very generous gifts from J. D. Rockefeller Jr, before and after the Amsterdam Assembly. The Institute arranges courses for theological study: but its main contribution consists of courses for laymen and women: specialist courses for laymen of different professions, who study their own particular difficulties, sharing their experiences with the help of scholars and theologians who have a clear perception of the demands of the contemporary world: specialist conferences have been arranged, amongst others, for social workers, educationalists, and psychiatrists: doctors, clergy, and marriage counsellors (on problems of marriage and the home): poets, painters, and musicians: artists, playwrights, and architects: newspaper men: sociologists: philosophers. Since the opening of the Institute in 1947 to the end of 1952, 2,076 people had participated in the courses and conferences, the largest groups being sent from Germany, Britain, Switzerland, Holland, France, and U.S.A.; while the Churches represented were Reformed, Lutheran, Anglican, United, Orthodox, Methodist, etc. The present charge is 12.50 Swiss francs per day: but in certain cases scholarships are provided.

Closely connected with the Ecumenical Institute is the

Graduate School of Ecumenical Studies which began in 1952. Directed by a Board of Theological Professors of different countries and in close co-operation with the theological faculty of the University of Geneva it seeks to give theological students an opportunity for advanced study of the specific issues arising in the ecumenical movement. The students from all over the world who live and work together for four and a half months are thus prepared for the task of bringing the inspiration of ecumenical ideas into the life of their own Churches.

Women in the Church

At Amsterdam the Assembly received a Report on the Life and Work of Women in the Church, presented by Miss Sarah Chakko, Principal of the Isabella Thoburn College, Lucknow. It was presented on the basic assumption that this subject was the concern of the Church as a whole, and not a problem for women alone. It referred particularly to the need of making much greater use of the experience of women in the central life of the Church, through their inclusion in Church Councils, and Boards where policy is framed and decisions affecting Church life as a whole are made. It invited the World Council and National Christian Councils to give a lead in this direction by the appointment of qualified women on to their committees, and as staff members in responsible posts. It also asked that attention should be given to improvements in standards of training, remuneration, status, and security of employment. It made it plain that the Churches are not agreed with regard to the admission of women to the full ministry; but the Commission desired that the whole subject should receive further careful and objective study.

As a result of the Commission's recommendations, an inquiry was made by the World Council into the work and status of women in the Churches of forty-five countries. On the basis of the reports received, an extremely important survey was prepared by Mrs Kathleen Bliss, entitled *The Service and Status of Women in the Churches*.[1] This work was the first of its kind ever produced. Besides giving an account of the actual service of women, and devoting a chapter to the ordained ministry, it contained two very valuable chapters at the beginning and the end on the interaction between Church and Society, especially as it affects the role of women in both. There is an interesting footnote to the first chapter. Mrs Bliss points out that 'whereas in the West theology is almost always a study pursued by clerics, in the Eastern Church, by long tradition, the majority of theologians are laity; thus a woman studying and expounding the Scriptures would not be suspected of sacerdotal aspirations'.

In the last chapter, Mrs Bliss points out that there has been a revolutionary change in the place of women in society; but that it has been left on the whole to secular thinkers and writers to try to understand this revolution. She deplores the lack of prophetic and imaginative writing from the Christian side – due, she says, at least in part to the division in the Churches on what they think about the place of women in the modern world and in the Church.

Here is a subject to which the World Council is bound to give continuing attention, and to call for something else than quantities of 'practical little books'.

1. S.C.M. Press, 1952. 12s. 6d.

16

NATIONAL AND LOCAL ACTION

'Almost incidentally the great world fellowship has arisen; it is the great new fact of our era.' That is how William Temple spoke of the ecumenical movement at his Enthronement in 1942 in Canterbury Cathedral. But what about the ecumenical movement in our own nation? in our own town, or village? The question is very important, for in order that the World Council of Churches may be truly alive the fellowship which it expresses in a world context must also find national and local expression.

National Councils of Churches

It is here that the National Councils of Churches have a special value. They exist already in a number of countries to facilitate common action by the Churches in evangelistic enterprise, in the promotion of international friendship, in stimulating a sense of social responsibility, and in guiding the activities of the Churches for the welfare of youth, as well as generally for the promotion of Christian unity within their own area.

It will be simplest to take as an example the Council which I know best, the British Council of Churches. It was founded in 1942, and was formed by an amalgamation into a single body of three agencies on which the Church of England, the Presbyterian, and the Free Churches were represented in a variety of ways. Its functions are much the same on the national scale as those of the World Council on a world scale. The basis of membership is the same as that of the World Council, with the exception that two bodies, belonging to one of three amalgamating agencies, which had not accepted the basis, viz. the Unitarians and the Friends, also belong. There are 118 members. It meets twice a year, usually for two days, under the chairmanship at present of the Archbishop of Canterbury. It has Departments for Education, Faith and Order, Inter-Church Aid and Refugee Service, International Affairs, Social Responsibility, and Youth: and committees on Evangelism and Rural Questions. It provides means for enabling the Churches to act together on matters of national importance or public interest; and to make representation to the Government as may be required. Thus joint representations have been made to the Government in recent years, after full discussion, on the religious and social problems of the new housing areas; on Federation in Central Africa; on the terms of reference of the Royal Commission on Divorce; on Gambling, etc. A Commission which it appointed on Broadcasting produced a valuable report, dealing with the issue, amongst other issues, as to whether the Churches should approve of discussions on the wireless between those who take a definitely Christian and those who take a definitely non-Christian point of view. (It recommended approval.) The Director-General of the B.B.C. and the Director of the Television Department have come before the Council, and explained the Corporation's policy, and welcomed discussion.

The Council has given a good deal of attention to the whole question of the influence of the cinema, and religious films. It concerns itself with the welfare of young Africans coming over to Britain, and has been in close touch with the Colonial Office about a National Advisory Panel being set up in connexion with the welfare of overseas workers. It was the means through which the Churches took their part in the Festival of Britain in 1951. It is also the means by which, through its Reports and Bulletin, *The Church in the World*, information is circulated to the Churches throughout Great

Britain. One of its two yearly meetings is usually held out of London – recently, for example, at Edinburgh, Liverpool, Cardiff, and Belfast, thus making a big impact on the local situation. Its International Department does valuable work. A policy for joint action under the title 'Christians and World Affairs' was produced by and became the subject of an animated discussion in the Council. The Council approved it in April 1951 and referred the seven points in its 'Programme for Action' to the constituent Churches. Each Church which approved the points was asked to commend them to its own parishes, congregations, and organizations for study and action. It has been responsible for a campaign of local inter-Church Bible Weeks, with the title 'The Bible Speaks Today', in co-operation with the British and Foreign Bible Society. It was responsible also for the British Conference of Christian Youth in Bangor, North Wales, in 1951, when 1,000 delegates, including 150 from the Commonwealth and other nations, attended. At this Conference there was common worship in various forms, including an opening service in the Tabernacle Presbyterian Church. But the realization that they could not receive Communion together came as a painful shock to many of the delegates, and resulted in an insistent demand for reasons why it was so, and for fuller information about their own traditions of faith and worship.

One of the most important and far-reaching ecumenical activities, however, under the care of the British Council of Churches is its Department of Inter-Church Aid and Service to Refugees, which raises large sums of money every year, interests great numbers of Church members, and arouses much local enthusiasm wherever there is a keen and energetic churchman or woman, equipped with the knowledge which the Department is only too ready to supply, available to lead and inspire fellow Church members. It is indeed here, in the opportunities for service and for generous giving, that the ecumenical spirit finds its most direct and forcible expression.

Personal Friendship

What about the town, and the village? What about the relationship of congregations and their ministers to one another? What can the ecumenical movement mean here?

The word 'ecumenical' certainly means 'universal'; and the ecumenical movement in its fullest range is a movement for the unity of the Church, covering the whole world. But, without forgetting the universal note, the word ecumenical denotes also (in Archbishop Söderblom's words) 'that spiritual attitude which reflects a deep consciousness of the fundamental oneness of the Christian Church as a whole'. It is the reawakening or creating of that spiritual attitude and finding ways of expressing that fundamental oneness that is the real problem which has to be faced. It is in this deep consciousness of oneness on the part of Christian people, and in a continuing 'spiritual traffic' between the Churches, that the heart of the matter is found.

The first thing that is necessary – and it seems so obvious as to be a platitude – is for the Christians in one place to get to know one another, to make friends with one another, to recognize, not the 'party', but the Christian link. Laity should get to know laity, and ministers should get to know ministers, as fellow believers and friends. Next, Christians thus getting to know one another should take counsel together in the carrying out of their common responsibility as Christians for giving a witness to the Kingship of Christ in their neighbourhood. It is not 'getting people to come to church' that is the point here, but presenting the Christian way, that is to say, letting those who have 'no time' for the Church, or are angry with the Church, or think it irrelevant, see the Church in action – ordinary men doing their ordinary work 'with a difference' because they belong to Christ's people, and also giving service to their fellow men for the same reason. We in our various denominations must come out of our isolation, and draw others out of their isolation, and through friendship with one another and prayer with one another for the guidance of the Holy Spirit, speak and act as members of the World-wide Christian fellowship. And this should be done, and could be done, whenever any two or three neighbouring congregations, one, say, Anglican, and the other Methodist or Presbyterian, have among their members some who are possessed by this ecumenical and evangelistic spirit.

Local Christian Councils

One of the means through which members of different Churches can work together and give their common witness, and take common action, is through local Christian Councils. There are many of these in Britain and in the United States, and other parts of the world. But here again it is best to speak of local Councils in my own country.

Their objects are to promote a fuller mutual understanding between the local Churches; to enable those Churches to take united counsel and action where their common interests and responsibilities are involved; and to give such expression to their common faith and devotion as may from time to time be found desirable, having due regard to their different usages and traditions. They include clergy and ministers and lay representatives elected by local congregations, with some co-opted members. They are most of them in touch with the British Council of Churches, and from time to time their representatives meet to discuss common problems. Much depends on the energy and personality of the chairman or secretary, or both.

An annual report of the Bolton Christian Council of

Congregations speaks of public meetings held about Federation in Central Africa; services in connexion with the town's celebrations of the Coronation; work undertaken by the clerical members, on the Council's behalf, in serving the interests of the large number of overseas students studying at the Technical College. 'Christian friendship has been offered to them,' the report says; 'help has also been forthcoming in finding suitable lodgings, and an excellent reception was given them in the Town Hall at the beginning of the autumn term.' There were open-air services in July and August; and a Bible Week was planned, with a large Bible Exhibition in the Central Library. This is only an example of the kind of activities in which a local Council engages. There are many more. Perhaps particular mention might be made of an unusual experiment in Coventry, where joint retreats for clergy and ministers have been held, in quiet surroundings outside the town enabling the different ministers to appreciate from closer experience the traditions, both in worship and biblical study, of the others. Information as to what local Christian co-operation means and how to achieve it may be obtained from the Secretary of the British Council of Churches.

There is an *Ecumenical Fellowship*, the object of which is to associate individual Christians with the work of the World Council of Churches and the British Council of Churches. The quarterly bulletin, *The Church in the World*, giving news of the ecumenical movement at home and abroad, is sent to all members who subscribe not less than ten shillings a year. Particulars of this may also be obtained from the Secretary of the British Council of Churches.

In addition to organized Councils, to which only the elected or co-opted representatives of different congregations can belong, there is everything to be said for joint general regional meetings from time to time, called by the clergy and ministers of the town or village, or group of villages. Such joint meetings may include only two or three neighbouring congregations; but what a new experience if numbers of those who pass one another's places of worship, as strangers, Sunday by Sunday, came together for counsel and prayer together about their Christian responsibilities in their particular part of the world. Work of a joint evangelistic kind is often undertaken. This takes various forms, depending partly on the kind of place in which the Churches engaged in this enterprise are situated, as well as on personal capacities. Sometimes there are a series of meetings, with united platform, at which speakers of different denominations deal with immediate human problems – marriage, the bringing up of children, juvenile delinquency, peace, race questions, capital punishment, Communism, and so on. Very valuable examples of such meetings were found in the 'Religion and Life' weeks during the war, sponsored by the British Council of Churches, and on some occasions shared with the Roman Catholics through their organization, 'The Sword of the Spirit'. It is sad that Roman Catholic co-operation is rather less forthcoming now than it was in war-time. But it may be that the Papal Instruction (to which reference was made in an earlier chapter)[1] may lead to further experiments in this country.

Courses of instruction, under joint auspices, on the essentials of the Christian faith are often of great value. And where there are new housing estates, or new towns, co-operation between the Churches is particularly important. In Crawley, Sussex, for example, there is a strong Christian Council, on which clergy and ministers and lay people work together to consider the social and moral and general development problems of the New Town. Indeed in this particular town a precedent has been set in a common approach by Anglicans, the Free Churches, and Roman Catholics to an Industrial Group representing the employers,

1. p. 72.

and to the local Trades Council, as well as to the Development Corporation, with a view to the mutual help of all parties in the building up of a community life.

For work and witness on most of these lines, and of course on many other lines as well, much can be learned from the experience of other Churches, Catholic, Protestant, and Orthodox, in other countries. There are reports as to possibilities, obtainable from the Evangelistic Department, the Study Department, and the Ecumenical Institute, all at Geneva; and help can be had from the British Council of Churches. There is literature available as well, especially in the chapter 'The Gospel at work in the World' in the second of the Amsterdam Assembly's preparatory volumes *The Church's Witness to God's Design*. Striking examples from Europe are the work of the French Protestant *Cimade* (pp. 152–4), and the French Catholic Worker Priests (pp. 155–7).

I have said nothing so far directly about 'Church Relations' in the more technical sense of the word. It has to be admitted that in Britain, as in other parts of the world, side by side with a growth in ecumenical fellowship, there has been a growth in the tenacity with which the churches maintain their distinctive positions. Personal relations between the leaders and members of Churches generally have however improved out of all recognition during the past forty years. Further, joint services, interchange of preachers from time to time, particularly on national occasions or in connexion with movements for promoting Christian unity, are by no means uncommon. There have also been a number of illuminating and useful conversations between representatives of the Church of England and representatives of the Church of Scotland, and representatives of the Church of England and representatives of the Free Churches, with a view to trying to find a basis for a greater degree of Christian unity. These conversations are still proceeding; and a particular proposal for negotiation between the Church of England and the Methodists is receiving the attention of an official Anglican committee. And though the circumstances of Britain differ from circumstances overseas, there is no doubt that union movements among the younger Churches must have an increasing influence on the attitude of the parent Churches, and especially among members of the younger generation in each. It is to me personally a deep disappointment that so little ecclesiastical progress has been made; and that Church *unity* is not regarded as the urgent and vital issue that it is, calling for costly action on all sides.

17

CHRIST THE HOPE OF THE WORLD

THE doctrine of the Sovereignty of God and the Kingship of Christ lies at the heart of the Christian religion. But the world is not yet obedient to God's rule, and Christ is not yet accepted as King. Here then is the question which we ask at the end. Will the world ever be obedient to God? Will Christ's Kingship ever be fulfilled? *Vexilla regis prodeunt.* But will his banners ever be carried to their goal?

It is as an answer to that question that the World Council of Churches offers 'Christ the Hope of the World' for the main theme of the Second Assembly at Evanston in 1954. The world in which this answer is given is full of false hopes, of fear, and of despair. The World Council is young, but it is not too soon for it to make a serious attempt to declare, in relation to the modern world, the faith and hope which are affirmed in its own basis, and by which the Churches live. And it declares that faith and hope in no spirit of complacency, or in self-fortification against the world's ideologies. It confesses Christ as its King, and the world's King too, by whom all ideologies must be judged.

The Drag of Despair

When it first resolved to adopt this theme, at Toronto in 1950, the Central Committee was well aware of the current drag of fear and despair. People drift on, as they have often drifted before, 'without hope in the world'. The cause of this hopelessness may be personal frustration or disappointment or catastrophe, or a crushing experience of human cruelty and injustice. This kind of despair finds a remarkable illustration in a poem by W.B.Yeats called 'The Second Coming', written at a time when the troubles of civil war in Ireland and the First World War pressed heavily upon him.

> Turning and turning in the widening gyre
> The falcon cannot hear the falconer;
> Things fall apart; the centre cannot hold;
> Mere anarchy is loosed upon the world,
> The blood-dimmed tide is loosed, and everywhere
> The ceremony of innocence is drowned;
> The best lack all conviction, while the worst
> Are full of passionate intensity.
>
> Surely some revelation is at hand;
> Surely the Second Coming is at hand.

But it is a 'Second Coming' of a new and terrible kind – the coming of the very opposite of Christ.

> A shape with lion body and the head of a man,
> A gaze blank and pitiless as the sun
> Is moving its slow thighs. . . .

As he watches he asks —

> And what rough beast, its hour come round at last,
> Slouches towards Bethlehem to be born?

It is a terrible vision of a time when all values have gone, and everywhere there seems chaos and darkness.

False Hopes

Again, when the Central Committee chose this theme, it was well aware that the world was full of false hopes. These hopes may be variously described. There are some who believe that the spread of a democracy without God, that is a democracy inspired by purely humanist ideals, will at long last achieve the perfect society. Such men holding the ideals of equality, freedom, and justice, but without belief in God, take little account of the frailty of the human factor. They also assume far too easily that in societies committed to the democratic way of life, none of these ideals is denied in practice. But inequality, discrimination, injustice, reliance on naked power, exploitation, and aggression are not absent from democracies.

Others believe that scientific humanism holds the key to the future prosperity of man. The ground of the scientific humanist's hope lies in man's past achievement. See, he says, with what astonishing success man has subdued nature! How marvellously he has developed his own mental powers, and created a specifically *human* world in the midst of nature – that is, a civilized society! All honour to the scientists, whose labour for the achievement of truth and the advancement of man is an inspiration to all. But civilization is the sheet-anchor of the scientific humanist's hope. If it disappears, then hope goes with it.

Others find the way to the perfect world in Marxism, with its appeal to the disinherited and to those who long to help the oppressed, to the more prosperous worker who feels frustrated in his work, and to the scientist and politician impatient for a new day. Marxism teaches that man has no fixed nature, but is continually being made and remade in history, which in turn by social action he helps to make. It is not only an analysis of history, but also a metaphysic and a religion. It shows history as a class struggle, which the workers, deprived of property, country, and family life, taught and led by a Communist Party, and united across national frontiers, can alone bring to an end by means of a revolution. Then (it is claimed) the golden age will come. Nature will cease to be man's enemy. There will be no more social classes, no class struggle, no coercive government, no cause for violence. All the wealth that mankind has amassed through the years will be made available for all.

These and similar prophecies have an undoubted attraction. Nor must the Church fail to confess its share in the sins which have helped to open the way for the Communist campaign. But there is another side to the picture – the methods employed by Communist leaders to seize and hold power in the name of the proletariat, and the explicit Communist teaching that any means required to break the hold of class enemies are justified. In practice, moreover, the Communist doctrine of the dictatorship of the proletariat has led in most cases to totalitarian dictatorship, in which the freedom of man is in fact denied. But more fundamental is the flaw in the Marxist creed itself: the rejection of God and his sovereignty, the unfitness of the actual proletarian as a Messianic figure, and the falsity of the expectation that sinful man as we know him can achieve, by mere stripping away of economic disabilities, a genuine resolution of historic strife.

The Christian Hope

It is in contrast with this despair and with these false hopes that the World Council of Churches proclaims 'Christ the Hope of the World'. The Christian hope is not 'a strong desire' for something which may be possible but is not certain. It is the product in us of God's acts in history, and above all of his act in raising Jesus Christ from the dead. Everything for the Christian centres on Jesus Christ. In Christ God fulfilled the hope of earlier times, and transformed it, in Jesus of Nazareth.

On the basis of the Bible, the Christian hope for the world can be seen to have two aspects. On the one hand, it calls men to acknowledge the ever-present rule of God, which means that man and the world have a definite purpose, that there are principles and standards for human society, rooted in God's everlasting will, for which men can work. There is something greater than the greatest of man's achievements, or even of his dreams, and the individual is not merely the product of his own efforts or of the discoveries of minds profounder than his own or of some impersonal process, but lives always as a son of God. For, in Christ, every man may know and work with the will of the Father, and be guided in all his efforts by the personal inspiration of the Holy Spirit.

On the other hand, there is nothing Utopian about the Christian hope. If the Church is not the Kingdom, no more is any human social order, however perfectly infused by the teachings of the Gospel. For God's Kingdom embraces the entire universe, and it involves, in the language of the New Testament, a new creation, a new world. It is always to this that the Christian faith points, and the Church confidently and surely preaches the ultimate realization of God's Kingdom in all its fullness because of its belief in the person and the work of Christ. In Him, the sting of all the evil in the world as it now is was drawn, the existing world-rulers of every kind were brought under God's rule, and there can be no reversal of this victory. In the future, men's highest hopes and profoundest schemes for society may come to grief as they have so often in the past. But this will not mean that they have been in vain, for it is to the establishment of God's Kingdom that they are directed, and this will at the last be achieved in God's own purpose.

We may now look a little more closely at these two aspects of the Christian hope, as they apply to the condition of the world today.

Here and Now

God's acts in history are not confined to the past. The power of the Kingdom which was at work in Jesus Christ is through the Holy Spirit continued in his people. Here and now, we believe, within the fellowship of his Church, is the beginning of the world to come, the first fruits of the new age, the transfigured heaven and earth. And there is not only a power given, but a duty laid upon us through the

Kingdom that now is. The Christian hope is a hope of our earthly calling. The difference between the Christian hope of resurrection and a mythological hope is that the Christian hope sends a man back to his life on earth in a wholly new way which is even more sharply defined than it is in the Old Testament. The Christian, unlike the devotees of the salvation myths, does not need a last refuge in the eternal from earthly tasks and difficulties. But like Christ himself ('My God, my God, why hast thou forsaken me?') he must drink the earthly cup to the lees, and only in his doing that is the crucified and risen Lord with him, and he crucified and risen with Christ.[1] The Christian hope bids men work for human brotherhood and justice, for racial equality and the peace of nations, for the fair distribution of food and shelter, for freedom from fear and want, from ignorance and disease. To accept Christ as the Hope of the World is to follow Christ's way in the world. To recognize Christ as King is to accept his rule for oneself and for society, and to be active in obedience to his will.

The Church as the pilgrim people of God is called to proclaim this Kingship, and to strive to be true to it in its own life. In the words of the Encyclical Letter of Pope Pius XI (*Quas Primas*), 'when once men recognize, both in private and public life, that Christ is King, society will at last receive the great blessings of real liberty, well-ordered discipline, peace, and harmony. If princes and magistrates duly elected are filled with the persuasion that they rule, not by their own right, but by the mandate and in the place of the Divine King, they will exercise their authority piously and wisely, they will make laws and administer them having in view the common good and also the human dignity of their subjects. The result will be order, peace, and tranquillity, for there will be no longer any cause of discontent. . . . If the kingdom of Christ, then, receives, as it should, all nations

1. Dietrich Bonhoeffer, *Letters and Papers from Prison*, p. 154.

under its sway, there seems no reason why we should despair of seeing that peace which the King of Peace came to bring on earth – he who came to reconcile all things, who came not to be ministered unto but to minister, who, though Lord of all, gave himself to us as a model of humility, and with his principal law united the precept of charity; who said also: "My yoke is sweet and my burden light".[1]

The New World

But the Christian hope points to a future at the end of history. The Kingdom that now is moves towards its full realization in the manifestation of God's through all creation. What we hope for is the fullness of what we already possess in Him. What we possess has its meaning only in the hope of his Coming. The character of the new age cannot be expressed in the language of ordinary prose. But the believer is quite sure that God's promises will be fulfilled, that the purpose of God revealed in Christ crucified will be seen, with a clarity that even the blindest cannot miss, as everywhere triumphant, and that 'the new life' in Christ will be fulfilled at the end of history. The New Testament uses the language of symbols, images, and pictures in describing this fulfilment; and the images used by New Testament writers have been all too often developed in fantastic ways. Images which are very revealing to some minds, or in some ages, may seem fanciful or even grotesque to other minds or in other ages. But the truth is greater than the form in which it is presented; and the truth is that the future lies with Jesus Christ'. 'The kingdoms of this world are become the Kingdoms of our Lord, and of His Christ: and he shall reign for ever and ever.' (Revelation 15.)

All we can be certain of is that as the past is Jesus Christ, and the present is Jesus Christ, so the future is Jesus Christ.

1. *On the Kingship of Christ*, 1925. Catholic Truth Society, pp. 12-14.

He is the same yesterday, today, and for ever. He who is both the beginning and the end, in whom all is to be consummated, is the One who meets us now and every day and invites us to commit everything to him. We do not know what are the limits of human achievement, of our own personal history, or of the history of the race. We do not know what possibilities are in store for us or what time is before us. We do know, however, that there is a limit, for we must all die. If we do not know Christ, death is the only limit we know. But with Christ death is transcended. He who has died for us, and is alive for us, confronts us with a totally new reality, a new limit, a new boundary to our existence. With him and in him the new world has begun!

GLOSSARY OF THE NAMES
OF CHURCHES

ANGLICAN CHURCH. A Church in communion with the Archbishop of Canterbury, basing its worship and doctrine on the Book of Common Prayer as authorized for its use in different countries or provinces.

BAPTIST CHURCHES. Protestant Churches which restrict baptism to the baptism of believers, usually by total immersion; and accordingly do not approve of the baptism of infants.

CALVINIST. See REFORMED.

CONGREGATIONAL CHURCHES (called originally INDEPENDENTS). Protestant Churches consisting of local and entirely independent congregations in free federation.

DISCIPLES or CHURCHES OF CHRIST. Originating in a split from Presbyterianism, they practise believer's baptism, and have a congregationalist organization.

EASTERN CHURCHES. Apart from those usually called simply 'Orthodox' (*q.v.*) there are other traditional Eastern Churches most of which use the word 'Orthodox' in their official titles: most of these Churches are identified with or closely associated with particular national traditions. Such are:

ARMENIAN ORTHODOX CHURCH (also called GREGORIAN after its evangelizer): head – Supreme Catholicos of Etchmiadzin.

ASSYRIAN CHURCH or CHURCH OF THE EAST: head – Mar Shimun.

SYRIAN ORTHODOX CHURCH: head – Syrian Patriarch of Antioch at Homs. One such Church is in South India.

COPTIC ORTHODOX CHURCH: head – Coptic Patriarch of Alexandria at Cairo. Closely linked with this Church is the

ETHIOPIAN or ABYSSINIAN CHURCH: head – Abuna at Addis Ababa.

FRIENDS. Society of Friends (also called *Quakers*) who reject all outward Church organization except 'yearly meetings'.

LUTHERAN CHURCHES. Protestant Churches, owing their name

to Martin Luther, which accept the Augsburg Confession of 1530 as their doctrinal basis.

METHODIST CHURCH. A Protestant Church which originated in the Evangelical revival led by John Wesley at the end of the eighteenth century.

OLD CATHOLIC CHURCHES. A union of six national Churches which accept the Declaration of Utrecht (1889) and are grouped round the ancient bishopric of Utrecht in the Netherlands. They reject the authority of the Councils of Trent and the Vatican, and the modern dogmas and other practices of Rome: and are in full communion with the Church of England since 1932.

ORTHODOX CHURCH. A Church representing the main tradition of Eastern Christendom, which derives from the Great Schism of 1054 dividing Eastern Christendom (with its chief See in Constantinople) from Western Christendom (with its chief See in Rome). But see also EASTERN CHURCHES.

PRESBYTERIAN. See REFORMED.

REFORMED CHURCHES (called also CALVINIST or PRESBYTERIAN). Protestant Churches claiming their origin from the reforms undertaken by John Calvin (1509–64), and professing his teachings.

ROMAN CATHOLIC CHURCH. The name given to the religious organization of all those who acknowledge the supreme jurisdiction of the Bishop of Rome (the Pope), recognizing him as the lawful successor of S. Peter.

UNITED CHURCH. A combination of Lutheran and Reformed in Germany: elsewhere sometimes refers to combinations of other Protestant bodies, e.g. United Church of Canada, and the Church of South India.

N.B. The word 'Church' as used of Member Churches of the World Council of Churches means not the whole of a denomination like the Anglican or the Methodist or the Orthodox, but an autonomous (i.e. independent or self-governing) Church belonging to the denomination. For example, the Orthodox Churches include such autonomous Churches as the Patriarchate of Constantinople, the Church of Greece, the Church of Russia, etc. Similarly the Presbyterian Churches include the Reformed Church of France, the Church of Scotland, etc.

STATISTICS OF RELIGIOUS ALLEGIANCE

IT IS impossible to arrive at a universally acknowledged standard by which to measure the number of adherents to different religions or different Christian communions. Thus the large figures assigned to Roman Catholics in the *Catholic Directory* normally arise from counting all those who have been baptized into the Roman Catholic Church as children, and even those who can be presumed to come from an original Roman Catholic family, or live within the boundaries of an established mission field – which results in an unrealistic picture regarding adult adherents. The calculation of Orthodox membership seems also to be based on a similar principle. If such a principle were applied to the membership of the Church of England in England, where 67 per cent of infants baptized are baptized in Anglican churches, we should have in England alone 27,569,118 members of the Church of England, out of a total population of 41,147,938 (1951). On the other hand statistics of Baptist membership are formed on the basis of 'believer's baptism', that is, of adults. The total numbers given on any computation must therefore be received with the greatest reserve: but granted this reservation, they may be regarded as a very rough index of the extent of the field covered at one time or another by the work of the respective Churches concerned, and especially of the proportion of Christians to non-Christians. The statement quoted below is from the *World Christian Handbook* 1952, published by the World Dominion Press, London. It is given by permission of the publishers. It would seem to be the best summary available and is consistent in itself.

The last estimate of the total population of the world in 1929 was 2,377,400,000. The total number of Christians is thought to be in the region of 700,000,000 but this figure is obviously not open to any rigorous check.

The Roman Catholics (*Catholic Directory*, 1952, p. 593) estimate the Catholic population of the world at 423,000,000.

No reliable figures are available for the Orthodox population of the world; the estimates vary between 144,000,000 and 172,000,000.

The Copts are said to number 10,000,000.

The figures claimed by some of the larger Protestant communions are as follows:

Lutherans: 68,500,000.

Presbyterians and Reformed: 41,100,000.

Baptists: community strength, 40,000,000 (Church membership 18,000,000).

Methodists: 30,000,000 (adult membership 14,360,900).

Anglicans: 30,000,000 (communicants 9,000,000), a serious under-estimate.

Congregationalists: 5,000,000 (adult membership 2,000,000).

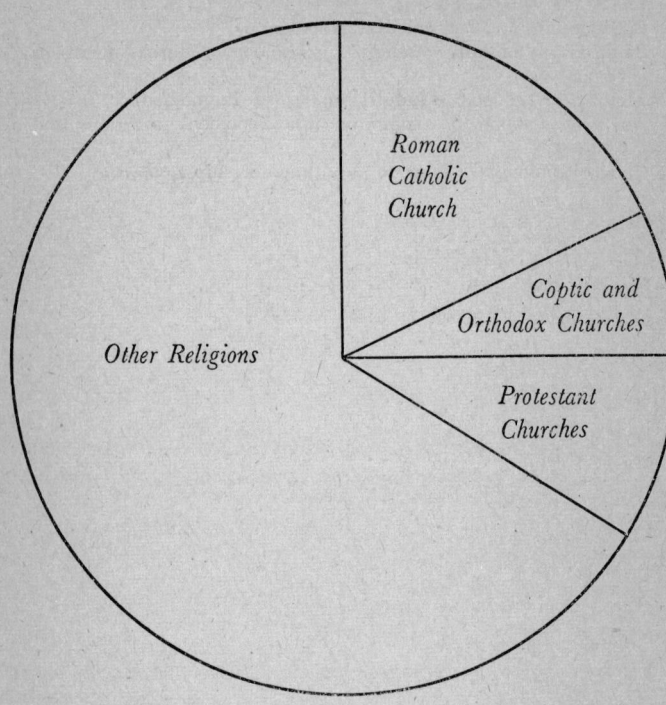

ESTIMATE OF RELIGIOUS STATISTICS (GENERAL)

Total population of the world (1949)	2,377,400,000
Roman Catholics	423,000,000
Orthodox and Copts	160,000,000
Protestants (inclusive)	213,000,000

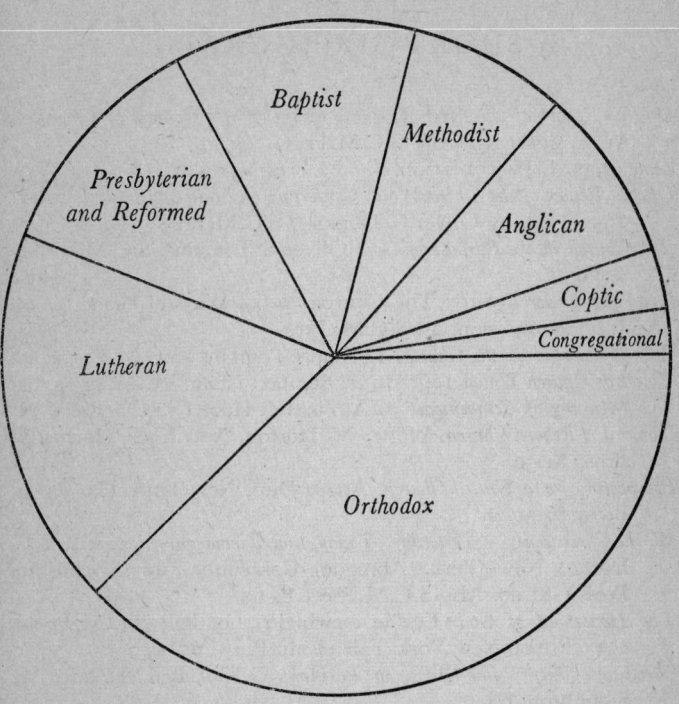

ESTIMATE OF STATISTICS OF THE LARGER CHURCHES
REPRESENTED ON THE WORLD COUNCIL

Orthodox	150,000,000
Coptic Christians	10,000,000
Lutheran	68,500,000
Presbyterian	41,000,000
Baptist	40,000,000
Methodist	30,000,000
Anglican	30,000,000
Congregationalist	5,000,000

APPENDIX III

A SHORT BIBLIOGRAPHY

Official Report of the First Assembly of the World Council of Churches. W.A.Visser 't Hooft. S.C.M. Press. 12s 6d.

Lund 1952. E.H.Robertson. S.C.M. Press. 3s 6d.

Official Report of the Third World Conference on Faith and Order (Lund, 1952). Ed. by Oliver S.Tomkins. S.C.M. Press. 21s.

The Church in the Purpose of God. Oliver S.Tomkins. S.C.M. Press. 2s 6d.

Faith and Order Reports: The Church. 3s 6d. Ways of Worship. 2s. Intercommunion. 2s. S.C.M. Press.

The Wholeness of the Church. Oliver S.Tomkins. S.C.M. Press. 5s.

Towards Church Union 1937–1952. Stephen Neill. S.C.M. Press. 6s.

The Meaning of Ecumenical. W.A.Visser 't Hooft. S.C.M. Press. 2s.

Toward a Reborn Church. Walter M. Horton, New York, Harper & Bros. $1.50.

Prospecting for a United Church. Angus Dun, New York, Harper & Bros. $1.50.

World Christianity – Yesterday, Today, and Tomorrow. Henry P. Van Dusen, New York. Abingdon-Cokesbury (for Friendship Press.) $1.00. Also S.C.M. Press. 8s 6d.

The Household of God. Lesslie Newbigin, London. S.C.M. Press. 12s 6d. Also New York, Friendship Press. $2.75.

Christian Unity: The Anglican Position. G.K.A.Bell. Hodder & Stoughton. 6s.

Ecumenical Foundations: A History of the International Missionary Council and its Nineteenth-Century Background. W.Richey Hogg. Harper & Bros. New York, and Edinburgh House, London. 12s 6d.

A History of the Ecumenical Movement. Ruth Rouse. S.P.C.K. 32s 6d.

Biblical Authority for Today. Ed. by Alan Richardson and Wolfgang Schweitzer. S.C.M. Press. 18s.

The Ecumenical Review. Published every quarter. Obtainable from Geneva, London or New York Offices of the World Council of Churches. Sw. Fr. 10; 14s; $3 per annum.

The Ecumenical Press Service. Weekly Bulletin of news and trends of opinion. Obtainable as above Sw. Fr. 15; 20s.; $5 per annum (reduced rates for clergy).

ADDRESSES

World Council of Churches:
Geneva Office: 17 Route de Malagnou, Geneva, Switzerland
London Office: 39 Doughty Street, London WC1
New York Office: 156 Fifth Avenue, New York 10, N.Y., U.S.A.

British Council of Churches:
General Office: 39 Doughty Street, London WC1
Inter-Church Aid and Service to Refugees Department: 5 Southampton Place, London WC1

Commission of the Churches on International Affairs:
20 Balcombe Street, London NW1
297 Fourth Avenue, New York 10, N.Y., U.S.A.

International Missionary Council:
Edinburgh House, 2 Eaton Gate, London SW1
156 Fifth Avenue, New York 10, N.Y., U.S.A.

Ecumenical Institute
Château de Bossey, Céligny, nr Geneva, Switzerland

*The following pages
contain descriptions of other
Penguins and Pelicans
of interest to
readers of
this book*

COMPARATIVE RELIGION

*

In recent years there have been remarkable advances in the study of this science, and much of the new material is passed on to the general reader for the first time by A. C. Bouquet in his *Comparative Religion* (Pelican A89, 2s 6d). The theme of this book is the religious quest of mankind, as manifested in many distinctive faiths, and in his analysis of these Dr Bouquet examines the reasons why they have maintained – or lost – their significance, and what are their prospects of survival in the rapidly changing modern world. Dr Bouquet has also written a new Pelican, a commentary on *The Sacred Books of the World*. Another authority on the subject is Christmas Humphreys, whose *Buddhism* (A228, 2s 6d) was described by *The Times Literary Supplement* as 'a welcome addition to the literature of Buddhism. Its able summary of all essential and up-to-date knowledge of the subject entitles it to be described as a pocket encyclopaedia of Buddhism.' The first volume to follow Mr. Humphrey's book in the Pelican Religions of the World series is *Christianity* (A269, 2s) by S. C. Carpenter who was Dean of Exeter from 1935 to 1950. He gives here an account of Christian origins, and of the evolution of Christianity to its present form, and attempts to assess the contribution that it is making or could make to the welfare of the contemporary world.

*

A STUDY OF CHRISTIAN ART

Byzantine Art

DAVID TALBOT RICE

A287

A century ago practically nothing was known about Byzantine art, and it is really only within the last twenty years or so that any except specialists have begun to pay attention to it. Yet its history extended over a period of more than a thousand years, the forms and motifs of early Christian art in the Mediterranean world furnished the basis for the whole of the European art that is familiar to us, and the influence of Byzantium on the West was not only of great extent, but also continued right down to the fourteenth century. The subject is thus one of fundamental importance to all who are interested in the story of European art and culture.

The book was first published by the Oxford University Press in 1935. For this new edition it has been revised from beginning to end, and some of the chapters, especially those on mosaics and paintings, have been completely rewritten. In addition, the results of all more recent research have been included – and in a field like this which has only received attention recently, new discoveries are numerous.

Though several similar introductions to the subject have appeared in foreign languages, this remains the only short book of its kind in English. It has sixty-four pages of plates.

3s 6d

The Brook Kerith

GEORGE MOORE

844

The basis of this imaginative story is that Jesus did not die on the Cross, but that he was saved from death by his friend the wealthy merchant, Joseph of Arimathea. The Roman centurion did not, in fact (the tale assumes) plunge his spear into the suffering body of Jesus, and was prevailed upon by Joseph to report that the execution had been carried out and that the victim was dead. Joseph was thereupon given permission to bury the body in his private sepulchre – but he carried Jesus off to recover on his secluded estate.

In the green pastures beside the Brook Kerith he works as a shepherd, and in the evenings joins in the ritual of philosophical discourse with the brethren. The climax of the strange chronicle occurs when Paul, a refugee from persecution, comes to this remote community, and discovers that Jesus is alive and has long renounced his Messianic claim.

It must be emphasized that this beautiful and reverent work of imagination is in no sense a perverse piece of religious controversy, and it is written with a delicacy of manner which will neither anger nor offend those who accept the Bible story of the life and death of Christ.

2s 6d

NOT FOR SALE IN THE U.S.A.

THOMAS A KEMPIS

THE IMITATION OF CHRIST

Translated by L. Sherley-Price

L27

After the Bible itself probably the best-known and best-loved book in Christendom is *The Imitation of Christ*, Thomas a Kempis's guide towards Christian perfection, which for over five hundred years has continued to exercise a widespread influence over Christians of every age and race. Unfortunately most English translators have tended to misrepresent this book – either by making unacknowledged alterations in the text to accord with their personal views, or by presenting it in a pseudo-Jacobean style. Thus many would-be readers have passed it by, and missed the advantage of Thomas's profound wisdom, his clarity of thought and vision, his wide knowledge of the Scriptures and Fathers, and his clear understanding of human nature and its needs. It was time for a new translation, and L. Sherley-Price, a senior Chaplain of the Royal Navy, has provided it for the Penguin Classics series. His, the first unabridged edition in modern English, presents a complete, accurate and readable version to the public.

2s 6d

...SPELS

E. V. Rieu

L32

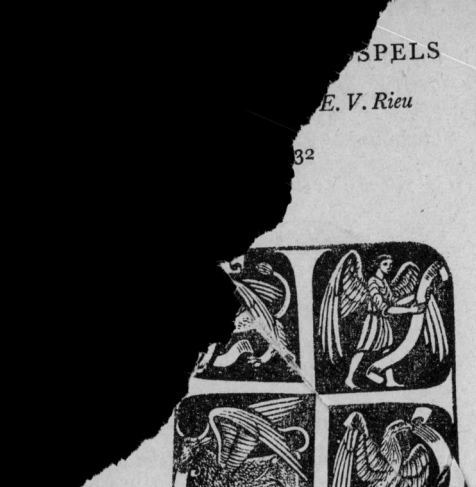

This is a new translation from the Greek, based for the most part on Codex Sinaiticus. It is an individual and independent piece of work. Those to whom the Authorized Version is a household word will be interested to see how much new light can be thrown on these, the most precious of all ancient texts, by the judicious use of recent discoveries in the field of paleography, and by their presentation in a contemporary style which aims at recapturing all the force and colloquial directness of the original. To others, the book offered as an invitation to look afresh at this venerable fourfold work; which the translator describes as the Magna Carta of the human spirit.

Dr Rieu, editor of the Penguin Classics series, has already himself translated the best-selling *Odyssey* and *The Iliad* by Homer, and Virgil's *Pastoral Poems*.

2s 6d

DANTE: TH[E

PART [I

Translated by D[

L6[

PART II: PUR[GA]TORY *will appear s[*

'A landmark in English publishing.' – *John o[* *Weekly*.

'Of all vers[e] translations of this poem into English, Miss Sayers's app[e]ars to me to be the most readable.' – *Time and Tide*.

'Encouraged by her almost loving guidance to a first careful reading of this Penguin, the proselyte will remain profoundly in her debt for a life-enhancing pilgrimage of the spirit through the most tremendous poem in the world.' — Sir Ronald Storrs in *The Observer*.

'I must say that I have had the most enormous pleasure from Miss Dorothy L. Sayers's introduction to her Penguin "Dante". It seems to me to combine a remarkable scholarship with an irresistible delight in the work in hand, which makes anyone who reads one page of it long to get down to reading the whole Comedy again.' – Sir Adrian Boult in *The Sunday Times*.

'It is a bold venture, and it deserves to succeed, for no pains have been spared, through commentary and diagrams, through critical introduction and glossary, to convey to modern man what it felt like to be in Dante's shoes.' - *The Scotsman*.

2s 6d ·

DANTE: THE DIVINE COMEDY
PART I: HELL

Translated by Dorothy L. Sayers

LC

PART II: PURGATORY *will appear shortly*

'A landmark in English publishing.' – *John o' London's Weekly*.

'Of all verse translations of this poem into English, Miss Sayers's appears to me to be the most readable.' – *Time and Tide*.

'Encouraged by her almost loving guidance to a first careful reading of this Penguin, the proselyte will remain profoundly in her debt for a life-enhancing pilgrimage of the spirit through the most tremendous poem in the world.' — Sir Ronald Storrs in *The Observer*.

'I must say that I have had the most enormous pleasure from Miss Dorothy L. Sayers's introduction to her Penguin "Dante". It seems to me to combine a remarkable scholarship with an irresistible delight in the work in hand, which makes anyone who reads one page of it long to get down to reading the whole Comedy again.' – Sir Adrian Boult in *The Sunday Times*.

'It is a bold venture, and it deserves to succeed, for no pains have been spared, through commentary and diagrams, through critical introduction and glossary, to convey to modern man what it felt like to be in Dante's shoes.' - *The Scotsman*.

2s 6d ·

THE FOUR GOSPELS

Translated by E. V. Rieu

L32

This is a new translation from the Greek, based for the most part on Codex Sinaiticus. It is an individual and independent piece of work. Those to whom the Authorized Version is a household word will be interested to see how much new light can be thrown on these, the most precious of all ancient texts, by the judicious use of recent discoveries in the field of paleography, and by their presentation in a contemporary style which aims at recapturing all the force and colloquial directness of the original. To others, the book offered as an invitation to look afresh at this venerable fourfold work, which the translator describes as the Magna Carta of the human spirit.

Dr Rieu, editor of the Penguin Classics series, has already himself translated the best-selling *Odyssey* and *The Iliad* by Homer, and Virgil's *Pastoral Poems*.

2s 6d